KATE MATHIAS

For Nora—
    May this year bring you much
happiness, good health, and lots of
laughter!

        Best wishes always,
            Kate Mathias
                xo

For more information, contact the author at www.katemathiasauthor.com
or follow her on Facebook at
https://www.facebook.com/WorldsApart.KateMathias

Interior Design by Angela McLaurin, Fictional Formats

Editing by Jim McLaurin

Cover Photography by Karen Scheffe

Cover Design by Shelly Pratt

Proofreading by Joleen First and Terry Trahan

DEDICATION

For **Stephenie Thomas and Kimberly Market—**
my sisters in fighting brain tumors.

And also to all of those who are still fighting,
those who have lost their fight, and those who are just starting
their fight. We are not alone.

Also, in loving memory of **Jeff Johnson—**
you lost your fight entirely too soon. You will be greatly missed.
May you rest in peace, dear friend.

Part of the proceeds of this book go to The National Brain Tumor
Society to help with research to find a cure.

Awake,
but still dreaming

PROLOGUE

I WAS HANDED my life sentence on February 10, 2014, the day I would have brain surgery to have my tumor removed. I wasn't wearing an orange jumpsuit; instead, a flimsy hospital gown engulfed my frail body. The tears flowed freely from my mom's eyes as my dad looked on with concern. All of my loved ones were there and huddled together, forming a semicircle around my small hospital bed. As I looked into my husband's eyes, I wondered if this would be the last time I saw him... the last time I hugged him... the last time I told him I loved him.

They each took turns saying their good-byes: my sister Liz, brother Bill, along with my sister-in-law, Shannon. My dear friends Shayla, Alexa, and Tanya were also by my side. I tried to reassure them with a smile, hugging each of them before being wheeled away. As I told them that I loved them, I wondered if these were indeed the last few moments of my life. I worried that I was taking my final breaths as the wheels of the gurney squeaked down the brightly lit hallway, slowly transporting me to the operating room.

But before I got to this point, I suffered through 16 months of illness—months that led up to this life-changing moment. This challenging experience has forever changed me and the ones I love. This is my story, my true story. One that I hope has a happy ending.

I knew that brain surgery would change me, but life has continued to change me ever since. Although I didn't choose it as one of my life moments, I'm grateful for what my brain tumor has given me, besides a hole in my head. (That was a joke. If you can't laugh at yourself, you'll never find true happiness.) Even in the darkest days of my journey, hope remained deep within my soul. I hoped that the person I used to be would fight her way back, out of the depths of darkness, depression, and pain. Humor has saved me as I continue on my journey back to that person, although I really don't know if I will ever be that same woman again. And, honestly, I'm learning that I may like the "new" me better, anyway.

My story is filled with sadness, despair, and, sometimes, soul-wrenching hurt. It is also bursting with inspiration, love, support, and—most of all—hope. As you'll soon learn, the dreaded "C" word doesn't stand for cancer in my house. No, it stands for *courage*.

ONE

My story
Sixteen months earlier

"WELCOME TO DES MOINES. It's a bit cooler than Phoenix at 73 degrees and the local time is 1:50 p.m. Thank you for flying with US Airways. I hope that you travel with us again soon." People started to shuffle as the muted ping sounded, signaling the seat belt sign had been turned off.

The plane was small, having only two seats on each side of the aisle. I waited silently as the people seemed to take forever to pull out enormous bags they had stuffed in the overhead compartments.

It'd been awhile since I'd seen my parents and was anxious for a weekend away. I needed a little down time and this quick trip was a perfect break from my busy life. My three children at that time were 9, 7, and 4-years-old, and my husband travels technically 75 percent of the time. It used to be that he was gone for two or three nights a week and then was home a week. Lately, however, his schedule had gotten so busy that he was on a six-week absence from home.

My husband... how can I describe this man father of my

children, my best friend? We've been together for 20 years, married for 15. We met when we were both 18 on the first day of our freshman year of college in the first class of the day. We were just friends for months before we started dating. He was a swimmer on the college swim team and very outgoing—or so I thought. I always joke that he tricked me in those early days because he talked all of the time. He's really an introvert and asks about everyone else to avoid talking about himself. Once Josh is truly comfortable with a person, he's actually very quiet. So naturally I have to talk twice as much as the normal person to make up for that. That's the excuse I always give him when he can't get me to be quiet. It works for us.

Josh is one of the smartest men I know. He finds the good in everyone and everything. If ever I have a weak moment when I'm complaining about someone, which happens more now after surgery, he's the first one to scold me.

He's a different man now than he was back then. But I'm different now, too. It's been *this* journey that has molded us into the people we are now—the couple we are now. We married at the age of 23 and have grown into adults together over the years. I always liked who we were as a couple before my brain tumor, but I like who we are now even more.

Josh is my rock. He never wavered in caring about me, loving me, and nurturing me during what would be a life-changing event— for both of us. He often had to pick me back up when I had fallen, both physically and emotionally, and would carry me when I couldn't seem to put one foot in front of the other. I'll never be able to repay him for all he's done for me, but I'll spend the rest of my life trying, and loving him. And for Josh and the person that he is, that will be enough for him.

This isn't your typical love story about a couple that meets, falls in love, falls apart, and gets back together. No, this is my true story about my journey with a brain tumor. There's nothing typical about a brain tumor.

Instead this story is filled with love—some heartbreak and definitely filled with hard times. But ultimately this *is* a love story and filled with hope. My life would never be the same as it was before the tumor—it would be better.

The aisle opened up in front of me and my thoughts were interrupted as I trudged off the plane and towards baggage claim. I was giddy with anticipation over seeing my mom. She was my ultimate cheerleader. I smiled, thinking that if I were half the mother she was, my children would be lucky.

I quickened my pace as I headed toward the escalators. Smiling at the Iowa T-shirts with corn and pigs on them, the University of Iowa versus Iowa State souvenirs in the airport shop windows, I remembered fondly this sweet place that had been my haven for my first 30 years. Making the move three years ago to Phoenix, Arizona, for my husband's job was a huge step for me, a huge step for my family. Still a Midwestern girl at heart, I now loved living in the desert and seeing the beautiful hues of oranges, purples, and reds splashed against the purest darkening skies as the sun sets on the mountains.

As I rode the escalator down, I saw her. Her white hair was cut in a bob and her blue eyes were shining. She was holding a handmade sign. It said "Kate Mathias Author of <u>Worlds Apart</u>."

Oh, good Lord. She didn't.

She held it higher as I got closer and I started to laugh.

"Did you see my sign?" my mom asked excitedly.

"Yes, Mom, couldn't have missed it!" After a big hug, we linked arms and walked through the small airport to the parking garage.

I was there for the weekend to attend my first book signing for *Worlds Apart* at Barnes and Noble Bookstore. It was my first book in The Silver Oaks Series and I was excited and nervous about what the weekend had in store.

Secretly loving the sign my mom made me but blushing on the outside, I pulled my bag to a stop while Mom popped open the trunk. My mom hadn't stopped talking since I got there, and I nodded my head trying to keep the topics straight as she randomly jumped from subject to subject.

"Hang on a sec. I need to text Josh." I pulled out my phone but she must not have heard me because she didn't even pause in the story that she was telling me.

A smile played on my lips as I half listened to what Mom was saying. She would surely repeat it again while saying, 'Stop me if I've already told you this.' I quickly thumbed a text to Josh to let him know I had gotten to Iowa OK.

Me: *Just landed in DSM. Luv u!*

Josh: *Have fun with ur mom. Luv u!*

This is how we did it. Josh had started five years ago to text me before he would take off for his trip and always text me when he would land in what city he was in. This sounds crazy, but with all of his traveling, some days I didn't even know what city he was flying to. My text would ping and I would look down and say to myself, *Oh, that's where he is!*

My friends would think that I was nuts for not knowing where my husband was, but when he travels as much as he does, I can't keep up! It was OK. His traveling worked for us.

It was the end of September and I inhaled the already cool air that signaled fall was already sweeping into the area. The grass seemed so green compared to the brownness of the desert. Yellows, oranges, and the shades of red had just started to sprinkle the trees. I missed the change of seasons a little but never missed raking the endless leaves that seemed to keep falling even when I thought I had raked up the last one.

"Dad is just finishing up work and I thought we could go to dinner and see a movie. Is there one that you haven't seen?" Mom asked while quickly changing lanes on the interstate. Her driving scared me and normally I would have offered to drive but had been suffering with a headache that just didn't seem to go away.

"I think the real question is what movie haven't you seen?" My folks go to every movie that comes out and my mom doesn't like a single one. It's a joke with my siblings as we try and guess why she'll think that the movie was horrible and to "not waste our money".

My mom is a little crazy, not certifiable, and I guess that's why I come by it naturally. I once went with her go see *Contact*, a space movie with Jodie Foster in it. I remember sitting through the previews and as our movie started to play, Mom leans over to me and whispers—let's be honest, the woman can't whisper, it's more like a quiet yell—"I hate space movies, don't you?"

I remember shaking my head, laughing and whispering, really whispering back, "This *is* a space movie, Mom!" That's my mom...

As we pulled into the driveway, I looked up at the large ranch-style house that loomed in front of us. It's not the house I was raised in but literally next door to the two story house I had spent my first 23 years.

My family owned three lots of land totaling an acre and a half. My dad is a veterinarian by training, but he is a jack of all trades who dabbles in everything. He had raised evergreen trees in the lot where their current house stood.

When I think back to my childhood, I'm flooded with wonderful memories. We lived on a small L-shape street where the few houses all had kids, and we all played together. I didn't care that most of my playmates were boys and most of them were my older brother's age. They treated me like a sister and took no mercy in teasing me or capturing me when we played cops and robbers.

After my dad would sell a tree, the huge tree spade would leave 6-foot deep ice cream-cone-shape holes in the ground. Often we would have friends over to play and the neighborhood kids would play a round of hide and go seek—in the dark. We had no streetlights to illuminate those holes, only the light of the moon.

I knew where each of the holes was located like the back of my hand and would quickly navigate between them, careful not to fall in them. Being a mom now, I think back to how dangerous it was to leave them like that, but back then I just thought of it as an awesome way to get away from the "it" person who didn't know they were there.

The person that was "it" would be in hot pursuit, right on my tail when I would hear the desperate cry, "Hrmph! Help! I've fallen in a hole!"

I would laugh, because let's be honest, I'm easily amused and just a little bit crazy, too. Skidding to a halt, I would walk lazily back to my trapped friend in the hole.

Yelling out to everyone else, "You can come out! Angie's caught in the hole!" I walked back and saw her eyes glaring up at me, reflecting from the moon.

Let me explain these holes. They were obviously cut out in the dirt and the trees' old roots poked out from the sides. We would all take turns pulling ourselves up and out by grabbing the roots. Dragging our bodies over the side of the hole, we would wiggle like worms until we were free of the hole. It was the perfect hiding spot if you knew which ones to hide in that were easy to climb out.

Angie was my younger sister's age and like a sister to me. One of my brother's older friends came and grabbed her wrist and yanked her out. This odd mix of childhood neighbors that played and grew up together would always remain close, even over the years.

"Kate?" my mom asked as she pulled into the garage and I watched as the little stoplight on the wall turned to red, signaling her to stop the car. Dad had installed it for her, because as I said earlier—this woman is a little scary driving. She's so distracted because she's constantly talking.

"Oh sorry. What did you ask?" I turned and smiled at my beautiful mom.

"I asked if it was OK to try a new restaurant? You pick the movie, too." She switched off the ignition and climbed out of her silver Honda Accord.

"Am I sleeping in the basement?" I asked.

"Yes, unless you want to sleep in Grammie's room?"

"No offense Mom, but that bed is horrible. I think I've slept on softer floors."

"It's practically brand new. I have the same mattress and it's comfortable."

"How old is it?" I pulled my small suitcase out of the trunk.

"Mom bought it right before she moved in with us so... let's see... 11 years old?" My grammie moved in with my folks while she was healthy, and she had just passed away a few years earlier. She meant the world to my kids and me well, to everyone in my family. She was diagnosed with cancer and given two to four weeks to live. She died a month and two days later. Grammie was the most generous person I have ever known and a woman full of Southern grace and class. I still miss her every day.

"Mom! That's not new or even close. Do you know how many dust mites probably live in there? Disgusting." I laughed and pulled the handle of my bag up.

"Don't roll it on the floor!" Mom shouted out.

"I know. Can't mess up the painted garage floor." I could eat off of her garage floor. It's a sickness, really. Often I would come out and see my mom in her red robe with boots on in the middle of winter. She would be scooping clean snow onto the garage floor so she could get the salt and muddy icicles off her epoxy painted gray floor with speckles. I don't think this is normal behavior but to me this is my mom and that's awesome.

I picked up my suitcase and winced.

"What's wrong? Do you have another headache?" Mom asked me with concern.

"Yeah, they're getting worse. Don't worry. I'll just take some meds and will be fine."

"Ask Bill about them," she encouraged, walking up the steps to the door that led from the garage to the house.

My brother Bill is a family physician in a city about 20 minutes away.

"I'll ask him when I talk to him. Is his family coming over this weekend?"

"They're gone, but I'll be bringing Emma and Will to your book signing."

Emma and Will are my niece and nephew. I adore them. They're the same ages as my boys. I set my bag by the steps that go downstairs and walked into the kitchen. On the island is a beautiful bouquet of flowers.

"Oh, those are pretty!" I exclaimed leaning down to smell the flowers.

"Read the card."

"Why? Did you already read it?" I grinned.

"I may have glanced at it because it was open, but would

never read your stuff."

"Uh-huh," I chuckled, plucking the small note off the clear stake in the flowers.

'We are so proud of you. Hope your book signing is a success. Love, Shannon and Bill.'

"Oh, that was sweet!" I quickly thumbed a text to my brother and Shannon thanking them for the flowers.

The phone started to ring and Mom announced that it was Dad calling.

"Hello, Bill," Mom answered with a smile on her face, "Yes, she's sitting right here."

I whispered, "Tell him to hurry up. I'm starving."

"She says that she's hungry and to hurry up. OK. See you soon."

I flipped open Mom's iPad and started looking through the movies to see what was playing that my folks hadn't already seen. I scrolled through the list, stopping on *Pitch Perfect.* I clicked on the trailer and immediately starting laughing at Fat Amy.

"This one looks good. Have you seen it?" I turned towards Mom and pointed to the screen.

Mom shook her head no and then answered as she was wiping up imaginary crumbs from the counter. Her kitchen was always spotless.

"I've never even heard of it," she replied.

"I remember something about it but think it looks good."

Now for the record, I hadn't ever seen *Pitch Perfect,* but since then I've seen it no less than probably 56 times. I still laugh at the horizontal running part and quite frequently answer Josh with a 'that seems like a good idea but betta not.' My kids watch it with us and many nights when we have carpet picnics where we have pizza on a blanket on the floor and watch *Pitch Perfect.* I saw Rebel Wilson once doing an interview and would honestly love to be around her for a day. I love to laugh and I think that she could give me some new material to tease Josh.

A few minutes later, my dad walked through the door. I smiled to myself as soon as I saw him. He's wearing a stripe short sleeve shirt with his "sweans" on. My uncle Wayne coined that term "sweans". Picture a combination of sweat pants and jeans... yep, an elastic waist and jean material. Growing up, my dad was always labeled as a clotheshorse. I remembered he used to have this old Iowa sweatshirt and I think he wore it nearly every day when I was a kid. It started to get a hole in the stomach so one day my mom put her finger in the hole and twisted. She was trying to take the poor thing out of its misery and help all of our eyes at the same time. She succeeded in ripping a much bigger hole but it didn't stop my dad from wearing the sweatshirt—it now just had a larger hole that we had to look at.

"Hey, Pops!" I smiled up at him and wrapped my arms around his large belly. My dad is about 6'2" and has a big belly. The rest of him is thin though. No butt and chicken legs. I guess I get that from him... the no butt part and chicken legs, although sometimes my daughter tells me that my stomach is fat and asks if there's a baby in there. Um, no, that would be called eating too much junk food.

My dad, also named Bill, has dark chestnut-color hair with only a little gray mixed in. He'll be 70 this year but still looks like he's in his early 60s. He has a funny little chuckle that shakes his belly when he laughs. I sound like I'm describing Santa Claus, and I guess in a way I am. Dad is one of the cheapest and most generous men I know. He's cheap (he prefers the word frugal) on so many things; like, he doesn't like to eat at nice restaurants and/or buy nice clothes, but he's so generous to family and strangers alike. If he sees a good deal on something he'll buy four of them and then give three away, sometimes to complete strangers. Dad would grab a gift out of his "prize room" and take, for instance, a green nonstick pan to one of my friends because he thought they would like it.

Dad is also the third William in our family. And as I've grown up, and my siblings have had children, it happens to take the guesswork out of naming their children. My brother is also William and goes by Bill. His son is William, too, but goes by Will. Six years later my sister had her first son and asked the family if it would be strange if she named her son William, too? When I heard about this, I encouraged it because I'm a bit ornery and thought it was funny. I don't think that my brother liked the idea much, but he never said so.

Growing up with two Bills in the house was confusing as hell. When people called it was always, "Do you want big Bill or little Bill?" Then for a short time my brother lived with us and it was "Do you want Dr. Bill?" That was a mess because both of them are Dr. Bill. So when my sister wanted to name her son William I was preparing for first cousins to have the same name.

Liz told my gram that she would probably call her William 'Liam'. My gram couldn't always hear the best and told my uncle that my sister's new son's name was 'I am'. I literally laughed out loud at that for quite a few minutes before I corrected her. Awesome. Just awesome.

In case you were wondering, Liz's son doesn't go by I am or Liam, but goes by William. My mom tried to shorten it once, and after Mom picked her head off the ground after getting it snapped off by my sister, she learned that his name is William. No nicknames.

So how does my mom feel about all of these Williams in the family? It's classic. And I quote: "Why does your dad get all of these boys named after him and I get no one? I did more to raise you than he did since he was always traveling. It's true that I don't really like my name anyway (her name is Carolyn) but they could've named the girls Caroline. That's a pretty name." Yes, it is, Mom. Yes, it is. I never encourage this conversation to occur or bring it up. I'm lying. Yes, I do, because it makes Dad and me laugh, or in my dad's case, chuckle.

"Let's go eat! I'm starving," I grabbed my purse off the counter, "Are we taking your car, Dad?" I asked hopefully.

Dad caught my look and nodded, "Yes, I'll drive. Did you pick out a movie?"

As the three of us walked to the door, I explained that we're going to a movie with singing that looks funny. He leaned over to me and whispered, "You know Mom's not going to like it, right?"

I laughed. Some things never change.

TWO
Barnes and Noble Book Signing
Still September...

MY PARENTS LEFT earlier that morning to go to my niece's basketball game. They were going to bring my niece and nephew to the book signing later that afternoon and have the kids spend the night.

The mornings in Iowa were so much cooler than I had at home. In late September, the temperatures in Phoenix were in the 90s. But it's a dry heat. That's what everyone says, and I laugh. It's still like putting your head in an oven but with no moisture.

I went on a quick run around my old neighborhood (let's be honest, it was more like a fast walk) to burn off the huge slice of cinnamon Bundt cake I'd had for breakfast.

Mom was a retired home economics teacher and always told me that home ec was the basis of all life. She could cook anything. Mom could make a piece of dried up leather taste good.

I don't cook. I mean, I do make dinners for my children so they can survive and all, but I don't cook like my mom. She was the type of mother who would have warm homemade chocolate chip cookies with milk waiting for us when we got off the bus after school. My kids get cookies, too... Girl Scout cookies (I bought nine boxes that year) and Oreos. Almost exactly the same as my childhood. Almost.

I didn't even break a sweat on my walk and actually was a bit chilled when I came up the driveway. Punching in the numbers on her garage keypad, I smiled to myself as my shoes squeaked across her painted, spotless floor. I glanced down at my watch and knew that I needed to get ready so I wouldn't be late to the signing.

Jumping in the shower, I turned my music up so I could jam out while I was getting ready. I'm not going into details about my shower because this isn't that type of book but I have to mention something that happened in the shower because it's an important part of my journey.

I propped my leg up on the edge of the tub to shave my legs. I was going to wear a navy pencil skirt and needed smooth legs. I leaned over and was slightly off balance when I felt a sharp pain on the right-hand side of my head. Slipping, I fell down in the shower and sat stunned as the water rained over my body.

I've struggled with migraines my whole life, but I've never experienced that type of pain before. I knew I had to get out of the shower. I grasped the handrail and pulled myself slowly up to a standing position. I wasn't finished shaving my leg but the few strips of hairiness would just have to do.

Quickly throwing on my skirt and buttoning my white blouse, I seemed to get my makeup on and fix my hair in a daze. Something felt off. I felt weird. Brushing those thoughts aside, I tried to convince myself that it was just nerves I felt worrying about the book signing.

As I drove to Barnes and Noble Bookstore, I thought about my life and how surreal it was that my book was in a major bookstore. It may not have been the lead story on the six o'clock news, but to me it was a pretty big deal.

I'm from a small town and only had 69 people in my graduating high school class. I was a fourth grade teacher for three years before giving that up so I could take care of my first son, Chase. I was a realtor for seven years and taught real estate classes on the side to contribute to my family's income so I could stay home with our kids.

It wasn't easy. Staying at home and taking care of my baby while working parttime was in essence a full-time job. My husband was working two jobs at the time and we were young, only 26 years old. Many times I would cry at night trying to figure out how to make ends meet. We would often have mac-n-cheese with Chase for dinner. A box only cost 79 cents and sometimes that was all we could afford.

I know all young couples struggle, and I'm not trying to make this a pity party but wanted to give my background. Josh and I worked hard for many years to get where we are. He stills works hard and has been traveling for work for seven years. It takes a toll on his body and makes it rough on me.

When we moved to Phoenix, I quit real estate because it was too hard for me to have a "normal" job with him gone all the time. We have never regretted our decision for me to stay home with the kids. Although we had to do without even small luxuries for about four years, it's was all worth it. I would do it again. Every. Time.

Many people have asked why I started writing in the first place. It was for me. This sounds selfish, but over the course of my life, everyone else came first. Even after I was married and became a mother, I have always been the person that doesn't say no to a friend when they ask for help—even if my plate is full. I run our household and take care of our children 80 percent of the time alone. I needed something for me. My daughter would be in school full time in the fall and I didn't want the time to come and for me to step back and say to myself, 'Now what?'

I needed to write for me. I needed to write so I could add another layer to what my children saw of me—what I saw of myself. I wanted to show them that not only was I their mother, a wife, a friend, a sister, a daughter, but I was also a professional that valued the education that I had worked hard for.

In January 2012, I started to write a story that I had been dreaming about for three years. It became *Worlds Apart*, which turned into the first book in my Silver Oaks Series.

As I pulled into the parking lot of the two-story bookstore that dominated the corner, I took a deep breath. I smiled and felt proud of where my life was going.

I shut the ignition off and swung open the door. I snatched my purse off the passenger seat and shut the door. As I smoothed my skirt down, I blew out a breath, and I headed into my first signing, not knowing what to expect.

Breezing through the set of double doors, I saw that they had set up a large white table on the right-hand side of the entrance. And there, in between two ladies, was an empty chair. On the table was a sign that read, *Worlds Apart* by Author Kate Mathias.

Holy crap! That was me. I am an author. I'm still not in the big leagues and haven't had the success like some of my Indie friends, but right now this was enough. I was enough.

I took my seat and introduced myself to the ladies on either side of me. All three of them seemed like pros at this. The two on my right wrote pet crime novels. And boy did those women know how to rock a pet theme. They stamped a paw print when they signed their books and passed out dog treats.

I knew they were dog treats because I was getting hungry and thought that they were cookies made to look like dog treats. I reached out and took one as I asked, "Can I have this, please?"

The redheaded woman answered, "You may, but don't eat it. They really are dog treats!"

Laughing, I said, "I'm so hungry that I may just have a bite. A small one. Don't tell anyone." I winked at her.

She chuckled and whispered, "Your secret is safe with me. So tell me about your..."

"Excuse me sir! Yes, you in the blue shirt. Do you like mysteries and tales of espionage?" The woman sitting on my left interrupted us. I won't use any of the ladies' names to protect the innocent or the slightly crazy; I mean that in the nicest way possible.

My eyes widened and I couldn't take my eyes off this woman next to me. I tried to look away but it was like an accident; I had to watch how this was going to play out.

The blue shirt man looked dumbfounded and slowly walked over to where we were sitting.

"Um. I guess?" he answered, unsure of the question that the lady had just shouted out to him.

"Sure you do. You need to buy my book. It has everything in it. Mysteries, espionage, intrigue. Here. Who should I make it out to?" She cracked open her book and held her pen poised above the open page.

"Err... Steve. My name's Steve," the blue shirt guy I guess named Steve answered.

"Great, Steve. I've made it out to you. Just take it to the counter and they'll ring you up." She snapped her pen closed and handed the book to Steve.

As Steve walked away, I fell back in my chair and must've had my mouth agape because my left-handed author (that's what I'm calling her to protect her) turned to me, "And that's how it's done."

"Whoa. I'm impressed," I said to Lefty. I really thought she was a bit insane but didn't want to say so because frankly she scared me a little.

"You have to be aggressive to get people to come over and talk to you. Just wait, I'll sell twice as many books as you. Just watch and learn," Lefty said.

This is ridiculous. Ridiculously awesome.

I sat up a little straighter in my chair, hoping to entice people to come and talk to me. I wanted to show Lefty that I didn't have to be pushy to sell my books.

The doors swung open and I saw a blur of people as new customers walked into the store.

"Excuse me! Sir! Do you like books about..."

Oh, good Lord!

I watched with interest and waited for the answer when the gentlemen shouted back, "No! No, I don't!" and turned and walked the other way.

A smile crept over my lips and I turned to the pet ladies to keep from busting out laughing.

"So how many books do you have out?" I asked the sweet author on my right.

She didn't answer but just lifted a finger to point at the front of the table where a woman was holding my book and flipped it over to the back.

"Oh, hi. I'm Kate. I'm the author," I mumbled out.

I didn't just say that. I think Lefty has affected me already.

"Hi, Kate. I'm Susan. Can you please tell me about your book?" The lady in the flower printed dress in front of me asked.

"Sure. It's a paranormal romance, technically, but doesn't have any witches, vampires, or stuff like that in it. It has a parallel reality that's happening at the same time," I watched her nod her head and hoped that she followed me.

"I don't believe in accidents. I think that everything happens for a reason even if you don't know what that reason is at the time," I explained. "The book has two women that look identical but one is a brunette and one is a blonde. They can jump into each other's worlds."

"Like with superpowers or something?" Susan asked.

"No, they don't have superpowers. They can just 'jump' into each other's world and at first don't understand why or how. They find that they need each other for different events that happen in their lives," I said.

"Well, Kate, that sounds different. I'll take one," she handed me the book to sign.

I smiled up at her and opened my pen. "It was Susan, right?" I asked her and hoped that I remembered how to spell and sign my name.

"Yes, it's Susan. Thank you," Susan took the book from me and smiled.

"It's my pleasure. Thank you, Susan," I grinned up at her and still had the goofy smile on my face as she walked away.

Take that, Lefty!

I looked over at Lefty and she was busy digging some imaginary important thing out of her bag on the floor.

More people were pouring into the store and I glanced down to straighten my books.

I heard Lefty take a breath.

And here we go!

"Sir! Ma'am! Do you like mysteries and espionage?"

"Why yes I do..."

I recognized that voice and looked up at my dad's smiling face.

Sorry, Lefty. These peeps are mine.

"That's my folks and my niece and nephew." I explained to

Lefty and started to stand so I could walk around the table and give the kiddos a hug.

"Oh—I hate children," Lefty sighed.

I looked at my dad and nephew who just heard her say that. Will's eyes got big and my dad got a look on his face that I had seen many times.

He's gonna try and make her be friendly, I thought. He's going to tell her jokes, and I can't wait to watch this all go down.

I scooted around the table and grabbed Emma and Will in a giant hug.

"Hey, you guys! How are my favorite niece and nephew doing?" They were my only ones at the time and are great kids.

Emma answered first, "Hi, Kate! Great!"

"How was your game, sweetheart? Did you score any baskets?"

"Yeah, a couple," her eyes lit up as she grinned.

"That's awesome, girl! How are you, Will?"

"Kate, did you hear what that woman said when we walked in with Grandpa?" Will asked, shocked.

I started to laugh and I heard my dad chuckle behind me.

"Will!" Emma exclaimed, as she is always appropriate. I swear she's like an adult trapped in a 9-year-old's body.

"I did, Will," I smiled at him and squeezed Em's shoulder. "It's OK. We can talk about it more at home tonight."

"I may have a joke for her," my dad started toward the table.

"Wait, Dad. You just got here. Hey, Momma," I hugged my mom and then wrapped one of my arms around my dad's waist. And then I felt a pop, and suddenly my bra was loose.

Oh, crap! My strap came loose! I knew I shouldn't have worn this bra.

"Um, I need to go use the bathroom quick. Can you watch my table for a sec?"

"I'll let Dad do that. I want to go check out Jeanne Cooper's autobiography. You know she's Katherine Chancellor on the *Young and the Restless*?" My mom quizzed me.

"Yes, I know," I said. Mom and I have been watching and recording Y and R for about 20 years. Even Josh will come in while I'm watching it and ask what Victor is doing. Guilty pleasure. "Go ahead, Momma. I'll be right back, Dad." I scooted off to the bathroom.

I ran into the ladies' room and pulled open a stall door. There was no way that I could fix my strap with my blouse on, so I had to unbutton my entire shirt. I hung it on the back of the door and had to take off my bra to fix the strap. I started to laugh to myself and wondered what Lefty would say if she knew I was in the bathroom having to get redressed.

I got myself all tucked back in and headed out to where the table was. More people were at the different authors' areas and my dad was leaning on the edge of the table talking to his mom. My grandma was 95 years old, and I was pleased that she made the effort to come out. My aunt Mary Jane and Uncle Bus had brought her to the store to see me.

My grandma was an ornery woman and once told me that she was going to live to be 110. I thought for a brief moment about letting my grandma loose on Lefty. I kinda wanted to see what things would fly out of my grandma's mouth.

"Thanks for coming, Gram," I said. I smiled at her and squeezed her arm.

"I wouldn't have missed it, kid," she grinned back up at me with her false teeth that she routinely took out in the middle of a meal and placed on the table. Once we were eating chocolate cake and the brown crumbs were caught in her teeth. She popped them out and on the table they went. I was slightly grossed out, but still continued eating my cake. I do love cake.

My daughter was only about a year and a half old, and she started to cry. Grandma scolded me and said, "See? She doesn't even know who I am!" We didn't see her often even though we lived in the same town.

I'm lying about how clear Grandma said that. It came out more like, "Seeee? Sha doesssn't evan knowww yew I am!" After all, she had no teeth in her mouth and now looked like the witch from *Hansel and Gretel*.

"Oh, she knows you, Gram. No one can forget you!"

She laughed at that, and I tried to calm Jillian by whispering in her ear, "It's not a witch. She does look scary with no teeth, but it's just Grandma."

I learned a lot of things by watching my Grandma. We had a strawberry farm and we sold strawberries in the summer from 8 a.m. to 8 p.m. every day. My folks believed in making us work at an early age—you know the good old-fashioned child slave labor—and I would be out picking strawberries when I was about 7 years old.

One day, the mosquitoes were really bad and after slapping one off my leg I saw my grandma waddling up to where I was standing. She had just come out of the port-a-potty. Those portable toilets always grossed me out. They were hot and steamy and smelled like ass; I guess because sweaty butts had been in there. Anyway, I looked up to see Gram had a big smile on her face like she had just done something grand.

"The bugs are bad today, huh Katie?" Grandma asked.

For the record, I hate the name Katie but I wasn't in the mood to tell Grandma to stop calling me that. She was old, after all, even then.

"Yeah, they're bad!" I waved my hand in front of my sweaty face.

"I have a little trick to stop them. You know that little white round thing that's in the urinal in the port-a-potty? I rubbed it on my ankles and it repels the bugs like nothing else!"

My eyes widened and I looked at her.

Did she really just rub the round deodorizer that the men urinate on in the port-a-potty on her ankles? Good Lord.

"Ummm. I'm not sure that's what it's supposed to be used for..."

"Sure it is. It really keeps the bugs away," she grunted and walked off.

I just bet it does and will keep everyone else away, too.

My book signing was the last function she went out in public to. She didn't make it to 110 years old. She lived a full life and died at the age of 98. My kids sometimes tell me that my cackle sounds like Grandma. I hope that I live to be that old and ornery.

I walked over to where Dad was telling a joke to the pet women.

Dad had won over the ladies like he always does. I smiled as I watched the pet women laughing at my dad for being him. He had always been able to diffuse a situation with humor and I guess he's where I got part of my sense of humor.

"Honey," Mom came up to me and said, "We're going to head home. I'm so proud of you and all of your accomplishments."

That's the thing about my mom. She has always been my biggest cheerleader in life and supporter. Growing up, I felt like I could do anything because she believed in me.

"Thanks, Momma. I'll be home later. Remember I'm having dinner with the Angies." I was meeting two Angies that I had known since I was a kid. Ang, I met when I was 5 years old and Angie, when we were in about fifth grade. Angie Clark would continue to be one of my closest friends during my illness in the days ahead. She would lift me up with her texts and would send flowers before my MRIs.

We always got together for dinner when I was back in town.

"Bye, Kate. See you later!" Emma said to me as they were leaving. I watched as they made their way out of the door. I was walking back around the table when I recognized a woman and stopped.

"Hi, I'm not sure if you remember me..." the dark haired woman said.

"I sure do! How are you, Mrs. B?" I asked. She was my childhood friend's mother.

"I'm great! Elizabeth told me that you were here today and she wanted me to come say hello."

We talked about our families and caught up. Her daughter was now a minister and she filled me in on what my friend was doing.

"I'd like to get a book signed," Mrs. B said, "and then after I read it, I'll give it to Elizabeth."

"Absolutely. It does have a few... um... scenes... adult scenes... it's not *Fifty Shades of Grey* or anything, but..." I shuddered out my sentence as I started to worry about the few steamy scenes in my book.

This was a minister's mother, for Christ's sake. OK, bad choice of words—still, this is a minister's mother!

I could feel as my face started to get hot as I grabbed a book and quickly signed my name in it.

Mrs. B chuckled, "It's OK. She does have three children and knows how that all works." She smiled at me to reassure me.

"If you're sure? It was wonderful to see you again."

"You, too. Take care," she gave me a small wave as she walked toward the cash register.

I glanced down at my watch and saw that it was five o'clock. The other authors were starting to pack up their things. I said my good-byes to the women and walked out of Barnes and Noble.

I sighed as I walked to my car.

That was fun. I'm grateful that I was able to have that experience.

I got into my mom's car and moved it across the parking lot. I was meeting my girlfriends at Rock Bottom Restaurant, which was in the same parking lot as the bookstore.

I swung open the door to the restaurant and saw Angie wave to me. I smiled at the girls as I walked over to the booth they were sharing.

"Hey! How are you both?"

Angie spoke first, "I'm good. How did the book signing go?"

I slid into the booth and threw my purse over to the side.

"Well, let's see... my bra popped off and I sold porn to a minister's mother..."

THREE

October 2012

I MADE IT home safely from my trip to Iowa and my house wasn't burnt down, so that was a good sign. Josh is always so good about letting me go away on the weekends and watching the kids while I'm away. He manages to keep them dressed and occasionally fed.

Now, in 2015, Josh is different when he watches the kids because he had to change. He had to help me when I was so sick, but back then it was a different story. My kids would tell me that they didn't get lunch or had hot dogs for every meal.

Chase would always say, "I don't even like hot dogs!" I would always laugh at the stories the kids told me when I got home. I secretly got pleasure out of seeing Josh collapse on the couch in a heap and exclaim, "I don't know how you do this!"

I'm awesome, that's how.

I quickly fell back into my normal routine of running the kids around, doing homework, laundry, burning the occasional meal, and writing. Josh was traveling as usual and I ran the house in my very OCD manner.

I've never been diagnosed with OCD, obsessive-compulsive disorder, but WebMD told me I have it. Josh is so proud.

The weather in Phoenix starts to cool off in the evenings in October, so the kids and I would go outside to ride bikes and play with the neighbors after dinner. We have a small Yorkie Poo named Molly and she would run up and down the street barking while Jillian drove her Barbie car around.

Oftentimes, my good friend and neighbors, Shayla and her husband Kris and I, would sit outside on lawn chairs and talk while the kids played. They have two girls and their oldest is Jillian's best friend.

Molly's barking filled my ears and I laughed as I watched Jillian not even watching the road, driving down the middle of the street.

"You're in trouble when she starts driving for real," Kris said and shook his head.

"No doubt. She's a terrible driver. Must get that from her grandmas," I replied with a grin.

"How have you been feeling?" Shayla asked me.

"I'm still struggling with headaches. I think my brother thinks I'm nuts, but he did tell me to go see a doctor about them. I'm scheduled for a brain MRI on Friday. What're they looking for with the MRI?" I asked Kris.

Kris is a colon rectal surgeon and is my self-imposed doctor. Bless that man. I've asked him stuff about everything. He never acts annoyed and helps me. Between Shayla and me, he puts up with all of the illnesses that we diagnose ourselves with.

"They are probably looking for MS spots or tumors."

"Tumors? Seriously? Do you think I have a tumor?" I asked him. Molly jumped up in my lap and I rubbed her back.

"No, probably not. You would have other symptoms if you had a tumor, like seizures. It's good to get it checked out though."

"Do you need help with the kids during your MRI?" Shayla asked me.

"It's during the day. Could Jillian come over to play for a bit while I have it?"

"Absolutely. The girls can play."

"Thanks, girl," I smiled over at my friend. "OK, kiddos: two-minute warning. We need to head in soon and get our showers," I yelled out to my kids.

As I drug the toys and riding things into the garage, I sighed to myself. Life was pretty damn good. The boys parked their bikes in the garage and walked past me on the way into the house laughing about something.

"Have a good night, guys!" I called out to Shayla and Kris and waved.

"You, too! Bye!" Shayla smiled as she was putting her chair away.

I pushed the button on the garage door and watched to make sure it closed all the way. As the door shut behind me I yelled out, "OK, stinky kids, in the shower! I can smell you all the way from here!"

Chase yelled in return, "Oh, good, then you got my present!" He was laughing from my room at having just tooted in the hallway.

Jillian was stripping off her shirt and looked up at me, wrinkling her nose. "Chase just tooted and it smells so bad!"

"Boys," I shook my head and laughed. "Right, sister?" We walked into my room together.

THE MRI WAS done on Friday and the scan went fine. I had lain perfectly still as the machine clicked and whirred. The knocking noise seemed to keep time to the pounding in my head. They told me that my results would be sent to my doctor.

It was Monday morning the 22ⁿᵈ of October and I had just gotten home from dropping the boys off at school. My cell phone rang and I glanced down at the screen that showed my doctor's office number.

"Hello?" I answered.

"Hello, may I please speak with Catherine?" the receptionist asked.

"This is she." Now again, I really don't like the name Catherine. I once asked my mom why she named me Catherine with a "C" when I spell Kate with a "K". She told me that it looked better with my maiden name. I guess she wasn't sure that I would get married... anyway, back to the phone call:

"This is Ocotillo Family Medicine calling. We have your results and would like to schedule a time for you to come in and discuss them."

"OK, great. When do you have appointments?" I asked.

"How about today at four o'clock?"

"Today?" I swallowed. A nervous feeling filled my belly.

"Yes, today. Does that work?"

"Um, sure. See you at four." I hung up the phone and immediately called Josh. He was somewhere traveling for work. It's not that I don't remember because of the mass in my brain. I often forget where he is because he travels every single week.

He picked up on the second ring.

"Hey, babe, is everything okay?" Josh answered. I rarely call him during the day especially when he's traveling.

"Hi. I'm not sure. They have the results and just made an appointment with me to come in to get them. They wouldn't give them to me over the phone. What's that mean?"

"Don't worry. Remember when I had to go in to get my cholesterol results? I think they make you do a visit for insurance purposes. I'm sure it'll be fine. What time's your appointment?"

"At four," I told him. "I need to see if Shayla can watch the kids for a bit."

"OK, sounds good. I have to head back into a meeting. Call me after your appointment, k?"

"I will. Love you," I murmured.

"Love you, too," he clicked the phone off.

I quickly typed off a text to Shayla.

Me: *Hey can you watch the kids tonight for a bit while I go to the dr to get results from the MRI?*

Shayla: *Sure! No problem. What time?*

Me: *Around 3:50?*

Shayla: *See u then! :)*

The rest of the morning blew by in a whir. I was coloring with Jillian and found myself staring off thinking about what they could've possibly found. And then I would switch to not worrying about it because like Josh said, it was probably routine to have me come into the office.

The boys got home from school and had a quick snack. I dropped the kids off at Shayla's house and drove the five minutes to my doctor's office. I climbed the flight of stairs to the second story of the brick building and walked up to the front desk.

"Catherine Mathias to see Dr. L please."

"Hello, Catherine. Could you please look over these forms and sign at the bottom if nothing's changed?"

I flipped through the papers on the clipboard and signed at the bottom making sure that none of my information had changed. I handed it back to the dark haired woman and smiled slightly.

"Thank you," she took the clipboard from me and immediately confirmed my information with a few strokes of her keyboard.

The door to the back rooms opened and a nurse stood there.

"Catherine?"

I stood and walked through the door that she was holding open for me.

"Hi, how are you today?" I asked the strawberry-blonde nurse.

"I'm good. Please step on the scale," she motioned with her hand for me to climb onto the scale.

I set my purse on the floor and then bent to take off my boots.

"Any little bit helps, right?" I grinned up at her as I pulled off my left boot and let it drop on the floor. I watched as she moved the black number square and recorded my weight on her paper.

"Follow me, please," she said, leading me into a room and pointed for me to take a seat next to the table.

"You can sit in the chairs. The doctor will be with you in a few moments." She turned and softly closed the door behind her.

I started to flip through the magazine that lay on the counter next to me. I couldn't concentrate on the words and just glanced at the pictures.

Why were my palms sweaty?

I wiped them on my jeans and started to bounce my knee.

The door opened and I smiled at my doctor as she walked into my room.

"Hi, Kate. How are you feeling today?" she asked as she took a seat on one of those stools with the wheels on the bottom.

"Hi, Dr. L. I'm about the same. I still have my headache. How'd the tests come out?"

"Well, the blood work all looks normal. Your thyroid levels are good and I think we'll keep your medicine the same," she was gripping two pieces of white paper and rolled her stool closer to me.

I looked at her with concern.

Why are you moving closer to me? What do you need to tell me?

"The brain MRI found something that is abnormal. You have a mass on your right frontal lobe."

"I have a mass? What's that? What does that mean?" I asked.

"I'm not exactly sure what it is until we can do further examination of it. I'm going to refer you to a neurologist," she stood and opened the door a crack. "Stacy, can you please call Dr. K and see if you can get Kate in to see him tomorrow?" Dr. L closed the door and came back to sit on the stool. Wheeling it closer to me again, she put her hand on my thigh. "What questions do you have for me?"

What questions do I have? How about am I going to die? What the hell just happened? What's this mass? What does it mean?

"Um..." I gulped. "I don't have any questions right now."

"OK, well, if you think of any, please call me and I'll answer them the best I can. The neurologist will be able to help a ton. Take care of yourself," she patted my hand, the one that was sweating and was gripping the jean material on my leg for dear life. She stood once more and then handed me the white papers from my MRI. "These are yours to keep. We'll send over your CD of your MRI to Dr. K."

"Thank you." I gazed up at her sympathetic face and felt my eyes start to fill with tears.

"You're welcome. My nurse will be in once she's set up an

appointment for you."

I watched her walk out of the room and studied the light wood paneling of the door. I felt as my body slumped over in the chair and a gasp escaped me. I lifted my hand up to my face and watched as it shook.

My other hand held those white papers that now had become wrinkled in my grip. My eyes scanned them reading the words MASS and RIGHT FRONTAL LOBE. Dimensions of the size of the mass were listed. One tear fell from my lashes and landed with a splat on the paper. My fingers were fast, quickly wiping the wetness away before it ruined the report. Another tear threatened to fall and I sat up straighter and took a deep breath. I needed to get back in control of myself. I had to drive home, and I have three kids that I still needed to make dinner for, do homework, give baths, and get to bed.

I have three kids. I have three kids.

I can't die.

My thoughts were interrupted as the nurse quickly stepped back in the room. "I was able to make an appointment for you for tomorrow at ten o'clock. Does that work for you?"

"I think so," I stammered. I took the card she was holding out to me with the neurologist's address and stood to leave. "Thank you."

I pushed open the office door and stepped into the cooler night air. As I gulped in the fresh air, I clumsily made my way down the flight of stairs.

What would I tell the kids? What would I tell Josh? My family? My friends? What was going to happen to me?

I pushed the button on my key chain and unlocked my door. I fell into my seat and cranked the engine, immediately calling Josh.

The phone rang and rang. When his voicemail picked up, I

burst into tears. I hung up the phone. This wasn't something I was going to leave a message about.

I drove the five minutes home in a daze with silent tears falling. As I bumped over the end of my driveway and waited for my garage door to open, I looked over at Shayla's house thinking about my children inside. Would I be around to watch them grow up? I couldn't stop the thoughts that slammed through my mind.

Was this a death sentence? How long would I have to live? Why was this happening to me and my family?

The car rolled to a stop and I got out slowly, collecting the papers off my lap. I clutched them in my hand and walked next door to pick up my kids.

I rang the doorbell and as I waited I couldn't stop the tears that were leaving a stream down my face.

Kris answered the door and took one look at me, "Oh, shit. Come in," he opened the door for me and I followed him to their kitchen table. I could hear my children laughing and playing upstairs. I'll always remember thinking that I wish that I could let them feel that way forever; that I would never have to tell them about what they had found in my brain.

Kris sat and motioned for me to sit next to him at the table. Later he told me that he was going to answer the door and say, "It's not a tumor," like Arnold Schwarzenegger, but once he saw my face he thought he better not. I actually can laugh about that now.

"So—what did they find?" Kris held out his hand for the papers that seemed to be glued to my palm.

"I have a mass on my right frontal lobe," my voice came out tiny.

Had I just said that?

And then Kris was Kris, the brilliant doctor and good man. It's like he went into nurturing mode.

"Alright, so it looks like they don't know much about the mass. The dimensions look like it's about less than a half-dollar in size."

"What does all this mean? Am I going to die?"

I was silently praying. *Please don't say I'm going to die. Please.*

"There's a lady in my office that had eight tumors in her brain. They were able to remove all of them and she is perfect, Kate, perfect. You wouldn't even know she had them. She had a long recovery for sure, but this definitely doesn't mean a death sentence. What are they going to do next?"

"I'm meeting with a neurologist tomorrow. I guess he'll do more tests?" I glanced down at the wood table and ran my fingers over the smooth, cool surface.

Jillian let out a scream and I could hear footsteps upstairs in what sounded like a game of hide and seek. I smiled weakly at Kris.

"What do I do now?" I looked over at him, tears still brimming in my eyes.

"Does Josh know?" Kris asked.

"No, I tried to call him but he must be in a meeting. Do you mind if I leave the kids here for a while longer and go try and call him again?"

"Sure. Take your time. The kids are fine."

I stood slowly and he followed me to the door. He opened the heavy glass door and patted me on the shoulder.

"Take your time," Kris smiled at me.

"Thank you. I'll be back soon," I returned his smile weakly and walked the hundred feet to my house. I punched in the numbers on the garage pad and pulled up Josh's number again on my phone.

It rang and rang and I walked into my bathroom while I was waiting. I sat down on my makeup stool and waited for the voicemail to go off. I hung up the phone and immediately called him back. That was our code that it was an emergency and so he would know to call me right back.

I hit end on the phone and looked at it in my hand. How was I going to tell the love of my life that I had a mass in my brain?

My hand started to vibrate as my screen lit up with Josh's picture.

"Hello?" I answered weakly.

"Babe, what's wrong? I stepped out of my meeting when I saw you called twice."

"I have a mass in my right frontal lobe... I... I... have a mass," my voice came out shaky as a warm tear ran down my cheek.

"OK," Josh paused and I could hear him swallow. "OK, what else did the doctor say?"

"I don't know," I was sobbing so hard now that I was having trouble breathing. "I have to see a neurologist tomorrow. J, I can't die. I just can't!" I bent over at my waist and held my stomach with one arm while cradling the phone in my right hand.

I don't know what Josh was thinking or doing on the other end of the line. We both sat in silence for a few moments, which seemed like hours, while this information sank in.

I'm dreaming. This is a nightmare. I'm going to wake up and my life will be like it was a few hours before.

"I should come home... I'm gonna come home," Josh spoke first and seemed to be talking to himself.

"No, don't," I insisted.

"Babe, I'm coming—"

"No. Stay and do your job. I'll have more information after I meet with the neurologist. You're going to be home in a day anyway. I'm OK. Really."

"OK, but if you change your mind, let me know. What did your parents and Bill say?"

"I haven't told them. I should call them now. I'll call you later," I said.

"OK, call them and babe—I love you."

"I love you. I'm OK, hon. Call you later," I half whispered.

I wasn't OK. Would I ever be OK again?

I inhaled a sharp breath and a sob caught in my throat. I needed to call my parents. Dialing my mom's number, I counted as it started to ring.

"Hi, honey!" my mom's happy voice answered me.

"Momma, I got my results back. I have a mass on my right frontal lobe—" I squeaked out.

"Wait. I'm having trouble hearing you. Dad and I are in a restaurant. Hold on, let us go outside," Mom said something to my dad about needing to go outside. I could hear shuffling noises as she was hurrying out of the restaurant.

"Honey, I have you on speakerphone. Dad's here with me. What did you say?"

"I got my MRI results back. I have a mass on my right frontal lobe."

My mom gasped and let out a little scream. I could almost picture her turning to my dad.

"What's this mean, Bill?" Mom asked my dad.

My dad's calm voice came over the phone. "Kate, what does the report say?"

I glanced down at the now familiar white piece of paper.

"It says, '1.8 x 1.6 x 1.5 cm heterogeneous focus of abnormal cortical and subcortical white matter T2 hyper intensity within the right frontal lobe exhibiting restricted diffusion. Findings therefore could represent an irregular area of unusual ischemic injury. A low grade cortical neoplastic process cannot be excluded with this appearance although there is minimal if any mass associated mass effect.' Dad, I'm so scared."

"I know you are, honey. And this is a scary thing. But it doesn't have to mean the worst. We need more information before we can come to any conclusions. What's your doctor suggesting you do now?" His words washed over me in a calming manner. My dad always knew what to say to make me feel better. Even when I was a little girl and I was at home sick, I would wait for my dad to get home from work to tell me that I was going to be OK. My mom was always the nurturing and loving one, physically taking care of me, but something about my dad's calmness had always been able to soothe me.

"I have an appointment tomorrow with the neurologist," I replied.

"OK, that's good. What did Bill say?"

"I've haven't called him yet. He's next on the list of phone calls," I explained.

"Honey, we love you. You're so strong and we'll get through this," Mom spoke up.

"I love you both, too. Momma, can you please call Liz and let her know? I'm going to call Bill, but then I have to go get the kids. And I'm not really wanting to keep talking about this," I said.

"I sure will. Please call us as soon as your appointment is over tomorrow," Mom asked.

"I will, Momma. Love you," I clicked off the phone and wiped the tears that had collected at the base of my chin with my palm.

I was emotionally drained but needed to call Bill and see what he thought.

As if on autopilot, I dialed his number and readied myself for the same conversation.

My brother answered the phone, and I could tell in his voice that he was tired. We don't talk much on the phone, and I hated to have this be the reason I was calling.

"Hey, Kate. How are you?" Bill answered.

"Hi, Bill. Hey, remember how you told me to go see a doctor when I got home about my headaches? Well, I just got my MRI results back and I have a mass on my right frontal lobe."

No matter how many times I had said that in the last few minutes it wasn't getting any easier.

My brother is a lot like my dad in his reactions and calm nature. He responded in a very doctorly way.

"What does the report show?" he asked.

I once again read the words off of that white piece of paper. I read the words flatly as if it weren't really describing me. I started to distance myself from this mass.

Maybe if I deny this is happening to me then it'll just go away.

"Is there any way that you can e-mail me that report? I'd like to read it," Bill asked.

"Sure, I'll send it over as soon as we hang up. Does this mass mean I'm gonna die, Bill?"

"It's too early to start talking like that. Let's wait and see what the neurologist does and see what he says about it first. OK?" Bill asked.

"OK."

There was that word again. OK... OK... but I'm not OK.

"Call me back if you have more questions later tonight. I'll be anxious to look at the report."

"I will. I don't even know what type of questions to ask right now. I'm sorta in shock or something."

"That's completely normal. Call me after your appointment tomorrow please?" Bill replied.

"OK. And thanks, brother." I pushed end on the phone and sucked in a breath that was raggedy from crying. I scanned the report and e-mailed it over to my brother and then typed up a text for the rest of my family and friends.

Me: *Hey all. I got my report back from my MRI. I have a mass on my right frontal lobe. I have an appt with the neurologist tomorrow. Will keep u posted.*

I hit send and my message flew out to my cousins, in-laws, and friends. Looking back on that now, it seems a bit crazy to write that in a text but I was already starting to distance myself from this diagnosis. It wasn't real if I didn't have to speak the words. I was dreaming—or no, I was awake, but still dreaming—more like living a real-life nightmare.

FOUR

October 23rd

I DIDN'T TELL the kids anything that night when I picked them up from Shayla's house. I figured that I would wait and get more information from the neurologist before I shared what the report showed.

My kids could tell something was wrong as soon as we were walking back to our house. Chase had asked me why I had been crying. It just made me cry more and now I had to try and hide it from my kids.

I wanted to climb into bed and go to sleep to escape what was now my diagnosis—my life. I had gone through the routines stoically that night. Usually, I have music playing in the background when I fix dinner, and I dance around and act goofy with my kids. I didn't that night. I couldn't.

When I woke up the next morning, I lay in bed for a few moments and stared at my white ceiling.

It was all a bad dream. I'm really OK.

I sat up quickly as a sense of relief washed over me. As my feet hit the floor, the pain in my head intensified and I let out a small noise.

Shit. It was all real. I need to get up and get the kids ready for school.

I rushed through my morning routine and dropped the boys off at school. As we were driving home from school, I glanced in the rear view mirror at Jillian.

"Sweetheart, you get to go to Shayla's house this morning."

"Yay! I want to play in their kitchen with Ansley. How long do I get to stay?" her sweet little voice traveled up to me from the backseat.

"I have a doctor's appointment, so you'll stay while I'm there."

"I want to eat lunch over there, Mommy."

"We'll see, honey. Do you want to play in my room while I get a shower?"

Jillian nodded, her blonde hair bobbing up and down in her ponytail. After I got out of the shower, I checked my phone to see what time it was.

"Huh. Aunt Liz has called a couple of times. I can't talk to her about this right now," I spoke out loud but it was really more to myself.

"What, Mommy?" Jillian looked up at me from her house she was playing with.

"Oh, nothing. You can keep playing," I smiled down at her and sat down on my makeup stool. Grabbing my phone off the counter, I flipped through my missed calls and text messages. I had missed a lot from last night, but I just couldn't talk to anyone about this right now.

My phone pinged in my hand and it was my sister again.

Liz: *Hey can you call me pls?*

Me: *I will soon. I can't talk now.*

Liz: *Ok*

My phone rang again and it was my mom.

"Hey, Mom," I answered quietly.

"Hey, honey. How are you this morning?" she asked with concern in her voice.

"Probably about as you would expect. I'm getting ready for my appointment."

"Have you talked to your sister?" Mom asked.

"No, she keeps calling but I just can't talk to her right now."

"OK, I understand. Please call her when you can though. She's worried about you."

"I know she is. I'll call her. I have to go, Momma. I'll call you later after the appointment."

"Sounds good. Talk to you later then."

I hung up the phone and sighed. Before I lost my nerve I quickly found my sister's number and hit call.

She answered promptly. "Hey, sister," her voice was quiet when she answered.

"Hey, I'm sorry I didn't call last night. I'm still trying to come to terms with all of this news," I explained.

"It's OK. I know it must be so hard. I'm here for you,"

"Thank you. I'm sorry I didn't answer all of your calls..."

"I was calling to talk to you about the mass but also needed to tell you something. I'm holding your new nephew in my arms. James was born this morning," Liz said.

"Oh, my gosh! Are you serious? I'm the worst sister ever!"

James was a month early, so naturally I didn't even think she could be trying to get ahold of me to tell me that he had been born. I was too wrapped up in my own stuff to have thought about anyone else at that moment.

Liz laughed, "Nah. Don't worry about it. I just wanted to tell you that you're an aunt again!"

In those few minutes I almost forgot about my mass. I drank in every word as my sister told me about James' birth, and I felt joy come back into my life. In darkness, there's always light that breaks through. James being born early and in the middle of my fears and struggles reminded me that good comes out of everything even if at the time I couldn't see what the "goodness" was in my mass.

About an hour later, I dropped off Jillian at Shayla's house and climbed back in my car to drive to my neurologist appointment. I pulled open the door and glanced around the small waiting room.

"Hi, I'm Catherine Mathias to see Dr. K," I explained to the receptionist.

"Hello, Catherine. Do you mind filling out these forms? I also need a copy of your driver's license and insurance card."

"Sure," I dug around in my purse for my wallet, "and you can call me Kate." I smiled at her weakly and handed her my cards. I took the clipboard from her and sat down so I could fill out my forms.

My head throbbed as I filled out my medical history. All of the crying last night hadn't helped my headache. I stood slowly and took my paperwork to the receptionist.

And now I wait.

I watched as the back door opened and a nurse appeared in the doorway.

"Catherine, er... Kate?"

I was the only one in the waiting room so I nodded and stood.

"Please follow me," she instructed and pointed to the scale, "and stop at the scale so I can get your weight."

Once again I kicked off my shoes and climbed onto the black step as I watched the numbers climb.

"Cute boots," the nurse said as she nodded her head to my black boots that lay next to the scale.

"Oh, thanks," I smiled as a part of me was thinking that I wish I could feel as causal as she was being like this was just a normal doctor appointment. I bent down and picked up my boots and carried them with me into the exam room.

As the nurse took my blood pressure, I glanced at the number she entered into her computer.

"That's high for me. I'm usually very low. I'm nervous," I explained.

She smiled and nodded, "It's understandable, dear. The doctor will be in shortly."

I sat and tried not to fidget as I waited for the doctor to come in. As the door swung open, I saw a short man with black hair walk into the room.

"Hello, Catherine. I'm Dr. K," the doctor explained and shook my hand.

"Hi. And you can call me Kate."

"OK, Kate, should we take a look at your MRI scans?" he asked. He slid the CD into his computer and adjusted the screen so I could see the images that popped up on the screen.

My eyes flicked between the doctor and the MRI images. I tried to gauge what he was thinking as he looked at my brain.

He cleared his throat. Pointing to the screen, he said, "Right here is the mass. Do you see it?"

I nodded and he continued on, "I'm going to order an MRA scan to check the arteries and vessels in your brain."

"OK, what will that show?" I asked.

"I want to see if there's any inflammation in the vessels

in your brain."

"What do you think the mass is?"

"Sometimes you can just have spots on your brain from old infections, or you may have had a small stroke."

Excuse me? What did he just say? A stroke?

"A stroke? But I'm in good health..." I stammered out.

"Let's just wait and see what the scans show. It's really too early to speculate. In the meantime, what else can I help you with?"

"I'm having really bad headaches lately." I explained.

He began to scribble something down on his prescription pad. "I'm going to have you try Imitrex for your headaches. Let's schedule to see you back in two weeks to go over the scans. That should be enough time to get them done." He stood and shook my hand before leading me to the frontdesk.

"Please schedule Kate to come back in two weeks. Also, please make an appointment at Marquis Diagnostics for an MRA scan, and let's also do one of her neck."

"Thank you, Dr. K."

He nodded to me and disappeared down the hall.

I made my appointment for two weeks later and walked out the front door to my car.

I had had a stroke or an infection? That didn't sound that bad. I had no lasting effects if I did have a stroke so maybe I was a lucky one. I felt OK healthwise, except for the daily headaches and the fatigue. The fatigue could be from taking care of my three kids a lot on my own and just from life.

On the drive home, I had convinced myself that a stroke wasn't the worst news I could've gotten and actually was starting to feel some sort of relief. I wondered if the immense pain I'd felt in the shower in Des Moines was when I had the stroke?

I'm lucky to be alive and have the only lasting effects be a headache. I was only 34 years old and suddenly felt like I'd be given a second chance at life. I started making all of the calls to Josh, my parents, my sister and brother, and they all went the same way.

"He thinks I may have had a small stroke."

Everyone's response was the same—a stroke? My dad and brother weren't convinced. They said that I didn't fit the typical candidate for a person that had a stroke.

I told them that I wasn't going to argue with the doctor. He knew best.

This was my first mistake. My body told me that wasn't the right answer, but my head didn't listen. I didn't want there to be any other reason I felt like this so I grabbed on to that diagnosis and cemented it in my mind.

Over the next few weeks, I had an MRA of the vessels and arteries in my brain along with an MRI of my neck. The whirring and clicking of the machine was starting to become very familiar.

During the days that followed I couldn't shake the feeling of being so tired all of the time. I also started to pull away from social interactions and from my friends. I got so I didn't want to talk on the phone, which for me is very unusual.

My kids are what kept me going. They are the reasons that I woke up every day determined not to let my health get in the way of their happiness. They could sense that I wasn't quite right and didn't complain when I told them that I couldn't do something because I was too tired.

Chase was the one that understood that I wasn't well more than the other two. Carter and Jillian were too young to understand what was happening with me. I couldn't stop the tears from forming when Chase would say to me, "Oh. You have a headache again? No, it's OK, Mom." I was letting down my kids and there wasn't anything I could do about it.

One night I was curled up in a ball lying on our closet floor. Josh came in and found me that way.

"Kate! What's wrong?" He practically shouted.

I was quietly crying.

"I can't do this anymore," I whispered between my sobs.

He crouched down beside me, "Baby, I know. I know you don't feel well. Do you think we can call your mom in to help?"

I looked up into his tired eyes. I knew that taking over for me because I wasn't feeling well was taking a toll on him with his travel schedule. Add on to it all the stuff that I usually did, and it was too much for one person to handle.

"I can't ask Mom. She's still at Liz's helping with the baby."

"I need help. I really need help. Can you please call your mom?" He quietly pleaded with me.

I knew in that moment that Josh needed help. He didn't want to ask for it, but he didn't have a choice.

I picked up my phone that was lying next to me on the floor and punched in Mom's number.

She answered in her cheerful voice.

"Hi, honey! How are you?"

"Hey, Mom, I hate to ask but can you come and help us? I know you're at Liz's, but Josh needs help and I just can't do much right now."

"Of course!" I could hear her quickly explaining to Liz what was going on. "Liz said that's fine. We are out to lunch with Jody now but let me know when you want me to come."

I nodded silently to Josh and mouthed *when?*

"I'll go look at flights right now. Give me a few minutes," Josh climbed off the floor and headed to his office.

"Josh is looking at flights right now. I'm so sorry, Mom. Can you please ask Liz if it's alright again?"

I could hear my sister in the background. "Tell Kate that it's fine. I've done this before and will be OK. Go, Mom!"

"She said it's fine. When do you want me to come?" Mom asked me.

"Probably as soon as you can... oh, wait, here comes Josh."

"I booked her on a flight that leaves in three hours."

"Three hours! Mom can you do that?" I asked.

"Sure, Liz, get the check; we need to go," I heard her direct my sister. "I'll text you when I land. See you soon, honey," my mom hung up suddenly.

"Is she coming?" Josh asked standing in the closet doorway.

"Yeah, she's heading to the airport soon I think," I paused, "How did you get a ticket that fast?"

"I used my points; otherwise it was over a thousand dollars. Traveling does have some perks," he smiled weakly at me.

We frequently took trips and I'm sure people were thinking that a) we are spoiled or b) we have tons of money and can afford to go on many trips. We are spoiled in the fact that we do get to travel a lot but it's not because we have a ton of money. Josh is gone so much that we have a lot of free airplane tickets. Last year he made 150 flights. Also, his hotel points start to rack up, too. So when we travel, we mostly just pay for our food since flights and hotels are paid for. That is quality time for our family since Josh misses out on so much of the kids' activities. I miss my husband every day but have gotten used to this life.

"MOM'S FLIGHT JUST landed," I called to Josh from the couch. "She just texted me."

"I asked Laurie to pick her up. I didn't want to leave you," Josh came over and ran his fingers up my arm. He looked down at me with a small smile on his lips.

Laurie is my cousin and she lives about twenty minutes from us. Over the next two years, she and her husband, John, would help out my family on numerous occasions by taking me to doctors' appointments, bringing meals, and watching my kids. I was so grateful for them.

I had put makeup on for my mom so I didn't scare her on how sickly I had started to look. I had dark circles under my eyes and they seemed lifeless. My spark was gone. I hadn't fixed my hair and had pulled it into a braid that hung on my shoulder after my shower.

I heard the garage door squeak open and Molly went running to bark at who I assumed was my mom and Laurie.

"Hi, Mom," I spoke weakly from the couch. "Thanks for picking her up, Laurie."

"Sure, it wasn't a problem," Laurie's soft voice came out.

Mom came immediately to where I was reclined on the couch. She perched on the edge.

"How are you, Honey? You look so pale..." I could see the worry in her eyes, her lips curved downward.

"I'm OK. Thank you so much for coming. I'm so sorry that I had you leave Liz's early," I glanced up to see Josh walk into the kitchen, "Josh needs help. I can't do it right now." I whispered so just she could hear me.

Mom patted my arm, "Don't worry. I'm here now. I'll take care of everything. Are the kiddos already in bed?"

"Yes, they wanted to see you, but since it's a school night Josh already put them to bed. They're excited you're here."

"Well, I am, too. Don't you worry about a thing. Your momma's here now and is going to take care of everything."

I sighed and felt a sense of peace and comfort wash over me.

I TRIED TO make life seem as normal as possible for my kids and even continued to post their funny stories on Facebook. I guess I felt like I could fake it until I made it.

"Kids, get your shoes on. We need to go get haircuts," I called out to them from the laundry room while I threw in another load of wash.

I could hear their grumbles of protest and smiled as Chase told his siblings not to complain because, "Mom isn't feeling well."

We all climbed into my SUV and headed to the salon right behind our house and put our names in. In this particular shop, they give out tokens for the kids after they get their haircuts to get a huge bouncy ball.

We already had a collection of these balls but the kids still wanted to get them every time we went in. Each child took a turn getting a haircut, and I watched as Carter held his hand out for his token.

Chase was still getting his hair cut, and Jillian and I both watched as Carter put his token in and a bright green ball came down the chute.

"Carter, you got your favorite color!" Jillian exclaimed.

Carter nodded and dropped his ball. I watched as it slipped through his fingers and hit the floor. It ricocheted off the tile and bounced into the shampoo display.

The woman at the counter gave me a dirty look, "Please don't bounce your balls in the shop."

"I'm sorry," I murmured and glanced over just as Jillian dropped her ball.

Again, it went bouncing all over and Jillian started to giggle. And then Carter dropped his ball again. Their balls were bouncing all over the shop!

I started to laugh and then caught the look of pure disdain on the woman's face.

"Oh, guys—stop bouncing those balls until we leave the store," I whispered to them loudly.

Chase finished up and now it was his turn to collect his bouncy ball. I quickly paid and watched as Chase's ball came flying out of the chute and shot across the floor.

Carter and Jillian must've thought now was the time to bounce their balls, too, and dropped them. Balls were bouncing all over the shop and the lady looked like she wanted to kill me.

Oh, good Lord.

"Guys, grab your balls!" I instructed.

"And grab your vaginas, too!" Jillian piped up.

I opened my eyes widely and stared at Jillian before I burst out laughing.

"Grab everything! Let's get out of here!" I pushed opened the door and ushered my kids outside where we were all laughing.

"I don't think that we're gonna be allowed to go back!" Chase said between laughs.

I snorted. It's an attractive quality I have when I'm laughing so hard that I can't help it.

"Jillian, I can't believe you said that!" Carter razzed his sister.

"What?" Jillian's innocent 4-year-old eyes looked up at me, "You told the boys to grab their balls. We don't have any, so I thought we better grab our vaginas."

"Good thinking, sister. OK, let's go home." I shook my head and rubbed my hand over my cheeks that were sore from smiling so much.

We've always been very open in our house and have called the body parts exactly what they are. This was the first of many discussions that would happen involving balls, penises, or vaginas.

That afternoon reminded me exactly why I needed to get healthier. I couldn't miss out on any more discussions like this. I couldn't afford to miss out on any more belly-hurting laughs. Little did I know in the next year, as my health would continue to worsen, that these laughs and the humor that I shared with my kids would be what saved me.

FIVE

Holes in my heart, literally and figuratively

NOVEMBER CAME AND brought with it cooler weather. It was like a switch went off on the first and suddenly the 100-plus degree temperatures were gone until the next summer. I felt like I could breathe again and started taking my dog on walks now that the pavement didn't burn her feet.

I had been back to my neurologist a few more times and the scans all came back normal for the inflammation. I was now having heart palpitations and a racing pulse so he referred me to a cardiologist. I also had joint pain so I needed to see a rheumatologist, too.

I joked to Josh that I was taking a tour of the doctors around Phoenix. We have only lived there for two years and I still wasn't familiar with where everything was.

I had an appointment with the rheumatologist that afternoon. I quickly dropped off Jillian at preschool and drove straight to my appointment.

I breezed through the door and blew a strand of hair out of my face. I glanced up at the clock and saw that I only had a minute to spare. The clock was next to a TV that was showing a program on lupus. It was talking about the different stars that had the disease. I found myself drawn in as they were talking about the symptoms. Some of them sounded so similar to what I was experiencing.

"Can I help you please?" the nurse asked as she slid open the glass window that separated us.

"Oh, yes, sorry. I'm Catherine Mathias for Dr. T." I automatically handed her my insurance card and driver's license.

She took the cards from me and in turn handed me a clipboard with forms for me to fill out. I took it from her and plopped down in the burnt orange chair, throwing my purse in the chair next to me.

I started to fill out the forms—they all started the same, but when I got to the part about heart history I listed a stroke.

"Wow, that feels real..." I muttered to myself. I continued to mark my other symptoms' boxes.

I'm a hot mess.

I started almost racing down through the boxes to see how fast I could fill this form out. Most of the boxes I was checking 'yes'. Fatigue? Yes. Joint/muscular pain? Yep. Heart palpitations? Uh, huh. The yeses were adding up, and I started to laugh in my head.

What's wrong with me? This isn't funny.

The nurse called me from the doorway shaking me out of my lunatic yes box checking. I followed her back to an exam room and waited as she took my blood pressure and temperature.

"Dr. T will be in shortly."

"OK, thanks," I swung my legs off the side of the table and waited.

Dr. T walked into the room and I smiled at the tall, thin woman that walked in and immediately shook my hand.

"Hi, Catherine. I'm Dr. T," she took my hand in hers and it was warm and soft, matching her personality.

"Hello. And you can call me Kate." I'm seriously cursing my folks for calling me Catherine in the first place.

"OK, Kate. So what brings you in today?" She sat down on a black stool and glanced up at me.

What is it about those stools? I'm starting to really not like them.

"I recently found out that had a stroke. My neurologist referred me here because I'm still having fatigue, pain in my joints that shifts every day, headaches, and just soreness all over," I explained.

"A stroke? You're so young and healthy looking," she said while flipping through my chart.

"I know, but I guess strokes don't discriminate. Oh, I also have a thyroid problem—Hashimoto's disease."

"How long had you had that? Hypothyroidism then?"

"Yes, for about five years. I thought maybe my medicine levels were off. What do you think?"

"Here's what we're going to do. I want to run a bunch of blood tests and check your THS levels, along with some other tests for other autoimmune diseases. Let's get some of these results and then go from here."

"Alright. Do I need to go somewhere to have my blood work done?" I asked.

"No, we have our own lab technician here. Follow me and we'll get the labs drawn. I'll call you with the results of the tests."

"Thank you." I shook Dr. T's hand and followed her out to where I was to have my blood drawn.

I smiled at the balding man in the white lab coat as I sat down in the chair and bared my arms.

"Let's see. This vein looks good. I need six vials today."

"Six?" I gulped.

"I'm good. You won't feel a thing."

I've heard that before! Josh would pass out. He hates blood.

I walked out of the doctor's office, my arm wrapped in pink gauze tape. And now I wait... again. I climbed into my car and rummaged through my purse for some Aleve. I popped two of those blue pills in my mouth and took a swig of water from the bottle that was in my cup holder. Today was going to be more of a migraine type of day.

WHILE I WAS waiting for the results of my blood tests, I was able to get in to see a cardiologist. I was anxious to see about why I was having heart palpitations.

I'm skipping ahead to being in the doctor's office because the waiting room and form completion is the same. The only difference I noted while waiting in the cardiologist's office was that I was the youngest patient there by far.

I was only 35... no, 34 years old.

Wait? How old am I?

I wish that I could blame it on bad memory problems as to not knowing how old I was, but no, I'm blaming it on Josh. As soon as I turned my next birthday, he would automatically change my age to another year older. My birthday is on Valentine's Day and so the very next day, he would say that I was nearly 35.

I silently cursed Josh when I came to the age part of the form. I honestly didn't know how old I was and had to count back from the year I was born.

The kids aren't helpful, either. We all had missed "meet the teacher" night before school started.

"I can't wait to meet your teacher, Carter," I had told him one night at dinner.

"She's old," he responded with a shrug.

"She's old? Like how old?" I asked.

Chase pipes in, "I've seen her and she is old, Mom. She's older than you and you're like 80."

Josh added, "Mom's not 80, but she is almost 40!"

Whatever. Now my comeback is I'm alive so my age is just a number.

Anyway, back to the form. I finally figured out how old I really was and was still thinking about that when Dr. C walked in.

"Hi, Catherine. I see from your history that you're having some erratic heart palpitations?"

I didn't correct him on my name this time because Catherine seemed more like an old person's name, and I was feeling like it today having not remembered my age.

"Yes, I am. The neurologist said that I had a small stroke sometime recently."

The doctor looked up at me, from yes—his damn stool—and raised one eyebrow.

"How did he determine that?"

"I have a mass on my right frontal lobe."

He pulled his lips to one side. "Hmm. Well, we need to do some tests before I think that can be determined. I'm going to have you fit for a Holter monitor to see if we can catch any of the irregularities. I'm also going to have you do the bubble test to look for any PFO's."

"What's a PFO?"

"It's a hole in your heart. When we're fetuses, we all have holes in our hearts. Most people's close when we are born because now our blood supply is separate from our mothers. Some people's never close. It's not a big deal in some cases, and we don't even do surgery most of the time anymore to fix them."

"How long do I have to wear the Holter monitor?" I asked.

"For 24 hours. My nurse will explain how to keep track of your activities. I'm going to schedule you also to do the bubble test. I'll see you back in my office after I have a chance to look at the reports."

"OK, thank you," I smiled at him.

He stood and gave me a toothless smile as he walked out the door. The nurse came back in and handed me a piece of paper.

"We've scheduled your appointment for Friday to get your Holter monitor on. The hospital will call you about the bubble test and get you scheduled," the nurse explained.

I took the piece of paper and glanced down at my appointment scheduled for ten o'clock on Friday. I checked out at the front desk quickly and scooted out the door. I needed to pick up Jillian and the boys from school. It was my car pool week when I also picked up two of our neighbor girls.

I drove quickly to Jillian's preschool and waited in the line to pick her up. I smiled at my little blonde pigtailed girl that skipped out of the room.

"Hey sis. How was school?" I asked her.

"Good, Mommy. We made turkeys for Thanksgiving. Are we going to pick up the boys now?"

"Yep. Right now," I grasped her tiny hand in mine and led her across the parking lot to the car. I unlocked the door and held it open for her. She climbed up into her booster seat and buckled her seat belt.

I clicked on the radio and the song *Timber* blared out from the speakers.

"It's Gigi's favorite song!" Jillian exclaimed. Gigi is what we call the kids' grandmas.

I smiled and looked at her in my rearview mirror. I listened as she sang out the words to the song—her voice pure and clear. We drove the quick five minutes to the boys' school and I pulled up to the curb to wait.

As I sat in the car waiting for the kids, I checked my e-mail. There was a message from my mother-in-law about Thanksgiving. Suzi and my father-in-law, Mike, were coming to my house in addition to Josh's brother, Justin, and his wife, Casey.

My eyes flickered over the message. They were coming in on Thanksgiving morning and leaving on Saturday morning. It would be a fast trip. Suzi is an awesome cook and I didn't mind having her take over my kitchen and do a lot of the cooking. I'm a total foodie but don't really like to cook. I'd rather clean.

I looked up and saw my kids walking toward the car. Carter and Danijela were racing toward the car. Chase and Adriana were walking slowly behind.

I glanced at my clock. 3:02 p.m. was displayed on the digital display.

Carter threw open the door.

"Hi, Mom! What's the time?" Carter panted.

"A new record! It's 3:02 p.m. I don't know how you guys make it out here so fast!" I exclaimed.

Danijela, Adriana, and Chase climbed into the car. I pulled away from the curb and headed toward our houses.

"How was everyone's day?" I asked as I drove the short distance to the main street.

"Oh, there's Ethan. Honk, Mom!" Chase pointed to the kid riding his bike.

I didn't have time before the window went zipping down and the kids were yelling out, "Do you know the muffin man?"

I laughed as Chase and Adriana were chuckling.

"I'm not even going to pretend to know what that means. Do you have much homework?" I asked.

"Yeah, I do," Chase sighed.

"Nope, just spelling," Carter said.

"First grade is so easy. Just wait till you get to fourth grade, Carter," Chase turned and explained to his brother.

I pulled into the girls' driveway.

"Have a good night, girls. See you tomorrow!"

"Bye. Thank you!" Adriana said as she climbed out and shut the door.

"Is Dad home?" Chase asked.

"No, not for a couple more days. Get a quick snack. Carter and Jillian have gymnastics tonight, so we need to get homework done before then."

I SAT PATIENTLY in the hard, brown chair waiting for my name to be called. A few days ago I received the results from the Holter monitor. It had shown that I did have a few irregular beats, but they wouldn't do anything about them just yet.

He wanted to see what the bubble test showed, and I was in the waiting room waiting to have that done.

"Catherine Mathias?" the receptionist called.

I got up from my seat and walked toward the small desk. I handed her my insurance card and ID and took a seat. She began quickly typing on her computer my information.

"And who is with you today?" she glanced up from her computer.

"Oh, it's just me. I brought myself," Josh was out of town again and I watched, as the look on her face became one of pity.

"OK, dear. It shouldn't be too much longer before they take you back," she smiled at me and returned my cards.

I sighed to myself. I was ready for the test to be over. I was walking back to my seat when the nurse pushed open the door. She called my name, and I walked over to where she was standing.

She brought me to a small room where a gown lay on the table. She closed the door behind us and pointed to the flimsy material that was folded neatly.

"Please remove your bra and shirt and leave the gown open in the front. The technician will be in shortly." The door softly closed behind her with a click.

I quickly removed my shirt and bra and put on the green gown. I wrapped my arms around myself as the room had a chill. I slid onto the vinyl table and waited.

The door pushed opened and two men walked through.

"Hello, Catherine. I'll be performing your bubble test today. We will be putting an IV in your arm and injecting it with saline. I'll be watching on the ultrasound machine to see if any bubbles escape when your heart pumps. Shall we get started?"

"Sure, although I hate IVs," I gave him a weak smile.

"We'll try to make it as painless as possible. B, can you go ahead and get her hooked up while I turn on the machine?" The man with the red beard turned and asked the other man.

I held out my arms for B to see. I watched as he gazed down at my blue-green veins protruding from my arms.

"Do you have a preference for which arm I use? You have some good veins," he asked rubbing his two fingers down my arm.

"I get that a lot," I smiled at him. "They usually use the left one but I don't care."

He took a swab with alcohol on it and began cleaning my left arm. He pulled the metal tray with the IV sitting on a paper sheet close to him. He took the tourniquet and wrapped it tightly on my arm. I watched as he readied the needle above my arm.

"This will pinch for just a second," he explained as he pushed the needle into my arm. He swiftly taped the IV in place and hooked up the tube that was connected to a syringe filled with saline solution.

"She's ready when you are," B prompted T. We both looked over at T as his hands stilled above the ultrasound machine.

"Perfect, I'm ready," he said, reaching for a bottle of gel. "This is going to feel cold for just a moment." T squirted some of the blue gel onto my chest where my heart sat beating strongly. "I'll try to keep you covered up as best as possible."

My gown shifted and exposed my breast just a little and I tugged it back into place. I turned my head toward the ultrasound screen and watched as my heart pumped and contracted in front of me.

"T, if you're ready, go ahead and inject the saline," B instructed.

"You're going to feel a cold sensation," T explained as his thumb slowly pushed in the plunger on the shot sending the saline into my IV. It did feel cold but wasn't uncomfortable.

I watched B's face as he was studying the screen intently.

"Ah," B grumbled and marked something on the screen and took some measurements.

My eyes darted from the screen to B and back to the screen.

What is he seeing?

"Um, B? What does 'ah' mean?" I was getting nervous watching him make measurements and pictures of what he was seeing on the screen.

"Just a moment, Catherine. T, we need to push one more saline through the line. I want to watch one more time."

I stared hard at the screen, determined to see what B was seeing. I didn't take my eyes off of the image of my beating heart even as I felt the cold solution pump once again into my vein.

"There. Did you see that, T?" B turned toward T and questioned him.

I spoke before he could.

"I saw something. Was that a few bubbles that just passed up?" I asked B already knowing the answer.

B cleared his throat and slightly nodded.

"I'm sorry. I can't discuss the results with you. Your doctor will receive this information and will go over it with you," B explained.

"I know what I saw, though. You can tell me, B. I won't say anything to anyone. Can you fix a hole in the heart?" I was nervous about what this meant for my health.

And I know... I shouldn't have asked but I wanted answers and sometimes when you ask you get them however right or wrong it is.

I watched as B swallowed. He glanced at T. He cleared his throat again, "I'm not at liberty to say, but if there *were* a hole in the heart it can be fixed with surgery."

T looked from B to me and sat quietly studying me.

"OK, fair enough. Thank you for the information. Am I done now?"

B made a few more clicks on the keyboard and then pushed his rolling chair away from the ultrasound machine.

"Yes, you're finished. T, do you mind removing the IV please?" As T slid the IV line out of my arm, he took a cotton ball and held it to the crease in my elbow.

"Do you mind holding the cotton ball for a moment?" T asked me as he stripped a piece of pink wrap off the roll. I held the cotton ball in place while he swiftly wrapped it around my arm where the

IV left a small hole.

I was exhausted today and had a bad headache. I let out a breath that I had been holding during the test and inhaled a deep breath of the fresh air as I walked outside to my car.

I quickly unlocked my door and slid into the seat. As I plopped my purse on my lap, I dug around for some Migraine Excedrin hoping to take the edge off my head. I shook the bottle and one lone pill came rolling out.

Hmm. I swore I had more pills than that left. I must've been taking more than I thought.

I cranked the engine and pulled out of my parking spot and headed home.

I activated my Bluetooth on my car.

"Voice," I spoke into the car speaker.

"Call Josh Mathias," I said clearly because it never understands what I'm saying.

"Calling Josh Madius using Kate's cell," the voice prompted back.

The kids always laugh when Siri says our last name. No one ever pronounces it right, including Siri.

"Hey, babe," Josh answered on the first ring, "I'm in between meetings. How did your appointment go?"

"Hey, so I think I have a hole in my heart," I explained changing lanes.

"What? And why do you sound happy about it?" Josh asked me.

"Because if that's the case, then they can fix it with surgery and I'll feel better. This may be what's causing all my problems. I finally have an answer," I explained.

"OK," I could tell Josh wasn't convinced, "What's the next step?"

"I'm not sure. I guess I just wait to hear from my doctor." I shrugged even though no one could see me.

"When is your next appointment?" Josh asked.

"On next Friday with the cardiologist. Wednesday with the neurologist."

"That all sounds good. Hon, I have to get back to my meetings. Call you tonight. I love you."

"Alright," I replied. "I love you—even if it's a little less because I have a hole in my heart," I laughed and pushed end on the phone call.

SIX

Is this really what my life is going to be like?

"DR. K WILL SEE you now," the nurse said as she held her clipboard. I followed her back into the neurologist exam room. I sat down in the armchair and waited for the doctor to come in.

The door pushed open and Dr. K walked through it.

"How are you feeling today, Kate?" The doctor asked as he came and took a seat on his stool.

"I've been struggling with joint pain where the pain moves from different parts of my body. Some days I can't hold my purse because my wrist is so sore. I'm also having a lot of headaches lately, and pain in my back and neck. What type of doctor do I need to see for this?" I asked.

"I can help you with that. I'm going to schedule an MRI of your neck and see what we can find," he explained, "I'm also going to have you try some new pain medication. You've tried Imitrex in the past; I think I want to try you on a new one. It'll help with the headache and the other pain." He scribbled a prescription on his pad, ripped it off, and handed it to me. "I'll have the front office schedule an MRI, and they'll call you to have it done."

I reached for the prescription and got out of the chair. I stood and followed the doctor to the front checkout area. Dr. K handed the receptionist his notes and asked her to set up an MRI.

The older lady with kind eyes explained to me that the imaging center would be calling me to schedule the MRI. I nodded my head and took the checkout sheet.

"The doctor wants to see you again in two weeks to discuss the results." We made an appointment for two weeks and I walked outside.

I quickly drove to the pharmacy to have my prescription filled before I had to pick up Jillian from preschool. Today would be a busy day getting homework done before gymnastics and the whole nighttime routine. My head was pounding as I waited in the hallway for Jillian. I closed my eyes and leaned against the wall trying to block out the noise from the other parents talking.

Jillian came bounding out of the room, her hair in a French braid, and was excitedly chatting about the science project that they had done that day. We walked through the door and Jillian immediately climbed on the small, brick wall that was next to the path to the parking lot.

"Let's get down, sweetheart. I don't want you to fall," I reached my hand out to her. She was walking along the edge like a tightrope walker balancing carefully. She grasped my hand and pain shot through my wrist. Today, the pain was in my left hand and arm. I shook it off as we walked to the parking lot.

Jillian climbed into her car seat and we headed to the elementary school to pick up the kids. As we drove, I switched off the radio. I couldn't stand the noise, as my head was getting worse.

All of the kids got in the car and they chatted about their day.

We drove the short distance home and I dropped the girls off at their house a few houses down from ours.

The kids rushed into the hallway and immediately threw their book bags in the laundry room and greeted Molly, who was barking and piddling all over. When she got excited she couldn't control her bladder.

"Everybody wash their hands," I called out to the kids, as I was the last one in the house. "How much homework do we have?"

Chase answered right away, "None for me. I finished mine in study hall."

"I have spelling and reading," Carter replied.

"I have no homework," Jillian voiced in a singsong voice.

"That's because you're in preschool. Just wait till you get in fourth grade. You're going to have homework then!" Chase responded right back to Jillian.

I noticed that I had a message blinking on the machine. I pressed the button and waited for the voicemail to start.

"Catherine, this is Dr. T's office. We have your blood results. Could you please call us to discuss them?" She said, leaving their office number.

I grabbed a piece of paper and played the message again. After I had written it down, I erased the message and picked up the phone.

"Who was that, Momma?" Chase asked.

"My rheumatologist. I need to call them back quickly, OK? I'll be right back out," I explained as I reached for the phone and took off for my bedroom.

I punched in the phone number and waited three rings until the receptionist picked up.

"Hello, thank you for calling Dr. T's office. How can I help you?" the receptionist answered cheerfully.

"Hi, this is Catherine Mathias. May I please speak with one of

Dr. T's nurses? They left a message that my test results were in."

"Of course. I'm transferring you back to a nurse. Hold please."

"Hello, this is Mary."

"Hi, Mary, this is Catherine Mathias. I had a message that my test results are in," I explained again.

"Oh yes, Catherine, thank you for calling back. I have your results right here," I could hear shuffling of papers, "Dr. T has reviewed your blood work and you have tested positive for Valley Fever and have four of the 13 markers for lupus," the nurse explained.

"OK, what does that mean, that I'm positive for Valley Fever?" I asked thinking that didn't sound good.

"It's common when you live in Phoenix with all of the dust. You probably had the symptoms and passed them off as a cold or the flu. It's a virus with no medicine that can be used."

"That makes sense but what about the lupus?" I knew a couple of people with lupus and although it was a kind disease most of the people I knew could control it with medicine and lifestyle changes.

"Your lupus isn't active. You have four of the 13 markers for it and Dr. T wants you to come back in two months to be tested again. That way we'll know if the lupus has activated. I'm going to transfer you back up to the front desk to schedule your next appointment."

"Thank you," my voice came out in a quiet whisper.

I had lupus possibly? Now I've had a stroke, a hole in my heart, and now possibly lupus?

I quickly made my next appointment and hung up the phone. I immediately searched for the symptoms of lupus on my phone.

My heart sank as I looked at the symptoms: joint pain and inflammation, headaches, chest pain (my palpitations), hair loss, and fatigue. There were a few more but they didn't apply to me.

No wonder I wasn't feeling well. How much illness can a person go through? Each day it was getting harder for me to function, but I had chalked it up to being tired doing all of the stuff with the kids when Josh was out of town. I thought my headaches and fatigue were from not getting enough sleep. I was feeling very alone and frustrated dealing with most of this by myself since Josh was gone. I was starting to feel sorry for myself. I considered myself to be a strong person most of the time, but couldn't help the vulnerable feeling that was pushing on my chest.

My shoulders slumped as I slowly turned the door handle and walked out to the family room where the kids were watching a show.

Chase noticed something was wrong right away.

"Mom? What's wrong? What did the doctor say?" he looked up at me as soon as I walked into the room.

"I'm fine, honey. They just wanted to give me my test results. I'll be OK," I said reassuringly.

Would I really be OK?

"OK Carter, let's get going on this homework. We don't have much time before gymnastics," I explained as I pulled his binder out of his bag.

I FELT LIKE I was starting to live in doctors' offices. I was back in the cardiologist's office to discuss the results of my bubble study.

Dr. C walked in and sighed as he sat down. He looked like he'd had a long day already.

"So the results of your bubble study came back, Catherine. Your heart looks good," he explained. Even if you have a small hole we don't do surgery on it anymore. The regulations have changed and it isn't beneficial to the patient to do surgery."

"Okay," I replied, confused. "I just found out that I have the markers for lupus. Do you think that's what causing my palpitations, then?"

"Lupus? Are you on medicine for that?" he asked.

"No, not for lupus yet. I am on some medicine for my headaches and pain, although it really isn't helping too much."

"Here's the thing... I've seen this a hundred times. You'll end up upping the amount of medicine you take because the amount of pills will no longer give you relief from the pain and your body will become resistant to the pills and need more. You'll end up in and out of the hospital because you'll get addicted to the pills. It's a never-ending cycle," he practically growled out.

"Alright," I choked out.

"I want to see you back in two months." He barely got the words out as he was already walking through the door.

I looked down at my hand. It was shaking and matched how I was feeling on the inside.

I was going to be in and out of the hospital? How was this my life?

I couldn't even drive home. I staggered out to my car and the tears started falling freely. I choked back a sob and realized that I needed help.

I turned on my car and immediately dialed my brother. I wiped off a tear that had rolled down my cheek and dangled on my chin.

"Hey, Kate. How did the appointment go?" My brother asked.

"Not well, Bill—I don't even know what to say," I broke loose and started crying harder.

"OK, relax and when you're ready, tell me what he said," Bill said, then patiently waited for me to answer.

I blurted out, "He said I'm going to have to up my meds because my body will get used to them and I'll get addicted to them.

The doctor told me that I'd be in and out of the hospital. Bill, this can't be my life. How am I going to take care of the kids in this pain and with Josh gone? I can't do it—I just can't..." my words came out watery as I tried to stop crying so I could explain to my brother what the doctor had said.

"Kater," Bill said, calling me by my nickname, "he's right that your body will become immune to that dosage, and so you'll need to continue to up the medication to get relief. But, you aren't going to be in and out of the hospital with addiction. You're stronger than that and don't have an addictive personality. You can do this. Your family is behind you, supporting you," he practically cooed to me. His words helped soothe me and I took a deep breath.

"OK," I sighed and stopped talking.

"Do you believe that you can handle this latest news and be confident that you can take care of you and the kids?"

"I don't know. I guess so," I whispered, my throat scratchy from crying.

"You are going to come through this. I know it, sis."

My brother helped me more than he knew that day. He helped me to believe in myself. Trust in myself. Become the fighter that I would desperately need to be in the next year.

SEVEN

Randy Brimhall

DURING THE NEXT few weeks, I became even more frail and tired. I was going downhill quickly and started losing weight. My headaches were getting unbearable.

I went back to the neurologist to get my results of the MRI. I had a bulging disk in my neck and he recommended a physical therapist to help me with my range of motion. I couldn't change lanes without turning my whole body.

I set up the appointment and went to my first PT session on January 2. I had never been to physical therapy before and didn't know what to expect.

Clearly, Randy, my physical therapist, had to think I was nuts when I walked into the clinic. I was wearing a light brown sweater, jeans, and boots. My hair went halfway down my back and hung in loose curls.

A man wearing a blue shirt with brown hair and glasses walked over to me. He extended his hand and I grasped it firmly.

"Hello, Catherine. I'm Randy Brimhall. Nice to meet you," he smiled.

"Nice to meet you, and you can call me Kate," I returned the smile and followed him back to a table. It was a large room and there were multiple tables set up around the space along with some exercise equipment.

"I'm going to assess you first. I need to take some measurements. What're your primary concerns?"

"I have pain in my back and mostly my neck. I can't really move it too well. It hurts to change lanes and I have a lot of headaches—like, every day. They never go away."

"OK, let's see how your range of motion is," he pulled my hair over one shoulder and started measuring using a protractor looking thing.

"Um, sorry about my hair. I'll wear it up next time..." I said sheepishly.

"It's not a problem," he continued to assess me.

I looked around at the other people in the clinic. They were all wearing workout clothes and on various machines. Some had their legs up in the air and a therapist was working on them.

I look ridiculous.

"I'm going to have you start on the arm bike for six minutes. Then Tyler will tell you what to do next," Randy instructed.

I followed Tyler over to the arm bike. He pushed some buttons until it came up six minutes on the display.

"OK, go ahead and start. I'll set you up on weights next," he instructed.

What the hell? I have to basically work out?

I began turning the wheels and started to sweat about two minutes in. My sweater all of a sudden got itchy and I was cursing myself for wearing it. I never really worked out. I walked occasionally but no weight lifting or anything too strenuous. I didn't want to pull a muscle—oh, wait, I didn't have any of those.

After I finished a half hour of exercises and was officially sweaty and my hair clung to my neck, I made my way back over to Randy's table.

"I'm going to assess the movement in your neck now," he explained, "Go ahead and lie on your back."

I did as I was instructed and Randy sat behind me on his stool. He held my neck in both hands and moved it in different positions to see how much flexibility I had.

"I'm going to go ahead and have you flip over on your stomach for a bit so I can take a look at your back."

"Do you mind if I take off my sweater? I'm dying from that workout. It's the most I've done in years. OK, I'm going to be honest, in my whole life," I laughed and he smiled.

"Go ahead," he waved his hand.

I reached up and grabbed my now drenched sweater and yanked it off over my head.

Please don't smell. Please don't smell.

I tried to do a sneaky armpit sniff (yes, girls do that, too) but I couldn't tell. I flipped onto my stomach and then I remembered what shirt I was wearing under my sweater.

Shit. Oh, shit.

"Uh, sorry about my shirt. I didn't realize I would have my sweater off," I felt my face get red and hot even though it was pressed in the hole in the table.

"No problem," his hands started moving over my back.

We have this restaurant called Oreganos that's one of our favorites. They have different sayings on their shirts like "Legalize Marinara" and Josh had bought me one that said, "Nice Haboobs" to support breast cancer. And yes, that's the shirt I was wearing. We had all laughed when Josh bought it, but after it went through the dryer it had shrunk a little. So now I was wearing a super tight shirt that said "nice haboobs" on it.

Real classy, Kate.

For people that don't live in the desert, a haboob is what we call a dust storm. A wall of brown dust and sand move across the desert in a slow wall. We always hope that a rainstorm to clean the air and anything that is outside follows it. The winds can blow up to 60 miles per hour and once picked up our glass picnic table and shattered it all over our backyard.

My boys like to call it a ha ha boobie.

Once we were going to soccer practice and we pulled up and I saw my friend Dave sitting on his tailgate with the hatch open. It was pouring but didn't seem to faze him. I pushed the button to roll my window down. The rain whipped inside and pelleted me in the face. Dave started laughing along with my kids in the car. I wiped my face off and held my finger up to Dave that I would talk to him once the rain stopped. We can get 2 inches of rain in five minutes.

Later after practice, Jillian said to me, "Mommy, I didn't like that big boob in your face."

"Hmm, what?" I asked her confused. And then I figured out what she was talking about. The ha ha boobie.

So as my face cooled down and I got over Randy seeing my shirt, I realized he was speaking to me.

"You have scoliosis?" he questioned me.

"Oh, yeah. A 10-degree curvature to the right. To be honest, it's the least of my problems," I laughed, "I have a mass in my frontal lobe that they think I had a stroke and I may or may not have lupus and a hole in my heart."

I could see Randy trying to process the information I had shared with him. I looked up at him as he was now standing on my right-hand side and speaking about how my joints moved and functioned. I'm sure that it was a riveting conversation but I couldn't concentrate on what he was saying.

There was an older man on the table perpendicular to me with his legs bent at the knees. He let out a quiet toot and excused himself.

Then he let all loose and the noise was flying out of him.

"Oh, shit! I'm sorry!" he was yelling in between noises. He laughed, "Oh, whoa! Whoa!" It sounded like maybe he needed to change his pants.

I was trying to hold back my laughter and it was hurting my face as I tried to concentrate on what Randy was saying. Randy never broke stride and remained stoic as he explained my joints to me.

How can he keep a straight face? Doesn't he hear the rumbling going on just a table away?

Later, after Randy and I were friends, I asked him about it.

"How did you not die laughing?" I asked him.

"I was. It happens all the time. And that's not the worst thing that's happened. For real."

When he finished what he was telling me, I sat up on the table as he explained that we were going to do TENS unit and heat on my back. TENS unit is an electrode that sends little electric shocks to your muscles to loosen them up.

As he was sticking them to my neck, I said, "Next time I'll dress more appropriately. Sorry about that."

"It's really no problem," he told me to lie back, "I'm going to schedule you for Wednesday if that's OK. Your doctor has ordered three times a week for now."

I lay back and he wrapped a heat pack around my neck.

I can totally get used to this.

He turned up the intensity of the electrode and I felt my muscles twitching along with the heat on my back.

"Oh, wow. This feels amazing."

"Good. I'll let you rest. I'm going to work on another patient, but I'll be back."

I closed my eyes and I fell asleep. I must've not known how tired I was. Taking care of the kids and not feeling well had taken a toll on me.

When I'm super tired sometimes I'll snort snore and wake myself up. It's a very endearing quality that I have, especially when I'm on an airplane and do it. Strangers will be looking at me with a smile assuring me that they just heard me snort like a pig.

The snort came out rather loudly, waking me up. I jumped and quickly looked around to see who had witnessed it. I couldn't move my neck since it was wrapped up.

Please no one be around.

"How are you doing, Kate? You just have another minute left," Randy was right next to me.

"Er... I'm fine. I must've fallen asleep. No worries; I woke myself up with my snorting," I rambled on. I have no idea what Randy thought of me that day with my craziness. He's gotten used to my awesomeness by now and has come to expect it from me.

I set up my appointments for the rest of the week and walked out into the bright sunshine.

"Well, that went well," I smiled to myself and shook my head.

EIGHT
Six months later

IT WAS THE end of July and school was starting on Monday. We live in a district that has a modified year-round school. I actually love it, as it's too hot in July and August to do anything outside anyway. The kids have a two-and-a-half week break in October, December, and March.

We were in Iowa during Meet the Teacher Night, so the kids didn't know what their teachers looked like. I had gotten their lists in the mail of the school supplies we needed.

I about went broke the year before buying all three kids supplies, so I got smart and we went to the Dollar Store. I was able to purchase most everything except the binders and the three-hole punched folders.

The school supplies were strewn all over the family room floor and I had the lists spread out in front of me.

"OK, Chase, grab the box of tissues, the three packs of glue sticks, and sharpened pencils," I said looking down at his list.

"Is that everything I need?" he asked.

"No, hang on..." We finally got all the supplies in the right child's backpack. I stacked them by the edge of the couch so they would be ready in the morning.

My little girl, my baby, was going to be in kindergarten this year. I couldn't believe that time had gone so fast. She was so ready to go though, as she was my third child and kept up with her brothers.

Josh always makes it a priority to be home on the kids' first day of school. The big day finally arrived and we were racing around trying to get used to the routine after being off for the summer.

I quickly pulled Jillian's hair into buns on each side of her head—like Princess Leia, she says. I dabbed some gel in each of my boys' hair and made it look "swag," as Chase called it.

We rushed out the door and everyone piled in the car. Our dog was barking at the door desperately wanting to come with us.

"Not this time, Molly!" Carter yelled through the door.

The doors slammed and I looked back at my three amazing kids.

"Everyone all set?" I asked and looked into their excited but anxious faces.

"I always loved the first day of school," Josh said, "You never have any homework on the first day of school."

"Dad, that's not true. I did last year," Chase responded.

"Are you guys excited to meet your teachers?" I asked. Chase would have his first man teacher this year, Mr. Janezic—or, as the kids called him, Mr. J.

Parents are allowed to do an environmental form and request specific teachers, explaining why we think a certain teacher would be a good fit for our kids. Chase really wanted Mr. J but didn't want me to request him. He had been so excited when he ripped open the envelope saying that he had gotten Mr. J for a teacher.

"I can't wait to be in Mr. J's class. He has a snake named Willie but it's really a girl. She's named after Willie Nelson when he thought the snake was a boy," Chase excitedly bubbled out.

"Oh, I know about the snake," I nodded my head. My friend Kelli wouldn't volunteer in his classroom because of the horrible fear of snakes.

"What about you, Carter and Jillian? Are you excited to see your teachers?" Josh asked.

"I know who my teacher is... she's super old and I've seen her yelling a lot at kids," Carter sighed.

I looked over at Josh. He could tell I was already worried. Carter is our sweet and sensitive boy. He's quiet until he's on his own with you and then won't stop talking. Chase often over shadowed him because of Chase's outsized personality.

"It'll be OK, Carter," I reassured him, "You'll be awesome with any teacher," I smiled at him.

"What about you, Jillian? Are you excited for kindergarten? You're a big girl now and will be at the same school as your brothers," Josh asked as he looked in the rearview mirror.

Jillian bobbed her head up and down, "I'm excited to see my teacher and make new friends." Jillian is a very easygoing child and has an infectious laugh.

Josh whipped into a parking spot and shut off the ignition. We lived only two minutes from the school and were there already.

"Let's do this!" Josh practically jumped out of his seat and opened the back door. "Slide out, Bud," he instructed Chase.

"We are all going to drop off Jillian first so you can show her where to meet you after school," I explained as we walked across the crosswalk. Although it was only eight o'clock in the morning, it was already 102 degrees. I could already feel the drops of sweat collecting on my lip.

"Why does Jillian get to go first?" Chase practically whined, "I want to go see who's in my class."

"Hang on, babe. This will only take a few minutes," we walked up to what is referred to as the kindergarten cage, which is actually a kinda disturbing name. It's a playground just for kindergartners that has a fence around it so they can't get out. So explaining it that way still doesn't sound any better!

We walked up and found her teacher, Mrs. Titchenal. She was an older woman with kind eyes. Her voice was sweet and she looked just like I thought a kindergarten teacher would look like.

"Hi, this is Jillian. I'm sorry we missed Meet the Teacher night," I explained, "We were out of town." I looked at the kids already in Mrs. Titchenal's line. They were all wearing black kindergarten T-shirts.

"Uh-oh. Were we supposed to get a class shirt?" I asked.

"Yes, but it's no big deal. I have extras. They're 10 dollars," she looked through her pile that she was holding. "I guess I only have mediums left," she held it out to me.

I started rummaging through my purse. "Do you have any money, hon?" I shot a look to Josh.

"No," he stated without even looking. He never carried much cash.

"Oh, here we are," I said and pulled out the last 10-dollar bill I had and handed it over to Mrs. Titchenal. "Thank you for the shirt."

She smiled and moved on to meet the rest of her students.

"OK sis, let's just slip this on over your clothes," I plopped it on and it was huge—huge like it hung down past her shorts. She held her arms out and then let them drop.

"Mom, c'mon. I want to go meet my teacher," Carter urged.

"Alright, Josh why don't you take Carter and I'll meet you over there?" I asked.

"Hey, Momma, I'm just going to go over to my line," Chase stated.

"Why? Do I embarrass you?" I smiled at Chase.

"No, but Dad does," Chase laughed and turned with a small wave.

"That's fine, Chase, but I'm still going to come over and say good-bye when I'm done with Carter and Jillian," I called after him.

I dug in my purse one more time, this time pulling out a hair rubber band.

"Turn around, sister," I took Jillian's shirt and bunched it up, tying it up with the hair band. "There. That's better."

"Mom, you'll have to shrink it in the wash," Jillian smiled up at me.

I laughed, "You got it!" I bent down on one knee and looked up at my little girl.

Don't cry. She'll get upset if you do.

I adjusted my sunglasses on my face and silently high-fived myself for wearing dark glasses.

"I know you're going to have an amazing first day. Be sure you listen to your teacher like you always do. I can't wait to hear all about it after school. You know where to meet your brothers then?" I gave her a big squeeze and didn't let go for a few seconds.

Jillian nodded, "Yes, Mommy. Bye!" She waved her little hand at me.

I blew her a kiss and watched as her line started walking into the school.

Where does the time go?

She turned just before she walked into the building and blew me a kiss. That's my girl.

I quickly turned to go find Carter and Josh. They were just a few hundred feet from the kindergarten cage.

"Hey, Bud; you found your line," I smiled at him.

Carter quietly nodded at me. I knelt down in front of him.

"It's OK to be nervous."

I looked up into his sweet face and Josh had his hand on his shoulder reassuringly.

"I see that you have a few friends in your class. That's fun. I'll see you soon. Have the best day! We'll pick you up afterward." I gave him a tight hug, "I love you."

"I love you 87 green M & Ms." That was our thing. We would find different ways to tell each other we loved him. When he was 2, he used to tell me that he loved me two chickens.

I remember my sister once getting that same response from him and I think maybe was a little offended. I laughed when she told me and explained that him saying that meant that he loved her a ton. Josh and I still text each other that phrase or 'I love you two poops' because it evidently is interchangeable.

"We need to go and say good-bye to Chase," I told Josh.

Carter grabbed Josh's hand.

"Bud, I'm just going to go say good-bye to Chase real quick and I'll be right back," Josh squeezed Carter's shoulder.

We walked in the sweltering heat over to where Chase was standing in the fifth grade line. Josh went right up to him and bear hugged him so hard that Chase was lifted off the ground.

"Dad!" Chase exclaimed, looking around to see who had seen him.

I laughed, "Put him down, Dad."

"I just wanted to embarrass him like he said I do," Josh smiled a toothy grin.

"Well, you did, Dad. Thanks for that!"

"I hope you have a great first day, Chase. I'm going to head back over and hang with Carter man until he goes in. He seems really nervous," Josh said.

"I think that's a good plan. I'll meet you over there in a few minutes," I smiled and pulled Chase into a side hug. He quickly pulled away. He had stopped holding my hand in public a few years ago. I understood it wasn't cool to be seen hugging your mom, but I didn't really care.

"I hope you have a great day. Don't forget to grab your brother and sister before you head across the crosswalk. I'll be waiting where I usually am."

"Got it. You can go now, Mom," Chase urged.

"Are you sure? I can stay until you go in," I looked around and noticed I was one of the only parents hanging around the fifth graders.

"No, I've got this. See you later!"

"OK, and Chase, I love you."

"I love you, too," Chase grinned at me and then started talking to a friend.

I walked over to where Josh was still standing with Carter.

"Man! When are they going to go in? I'm sweating to death out here," I complained and looked over just as a sweat drop dripped off Josh's brow.

Josh reached up and wiped his hand over his forehead, "You aren't kidding."

"Oh, look, we're going in," Carter pointed as his line started to move slowly toward the building.

"Bye, Bud! We're proud of you!" Josh called to Carter. That's Josh's thing with the kids. He tells them at night when they're going to bed that he's proud of them. Carter usually responds, "I'm proud of you!" Our sweet little boy...

I smiled and waved at Carter as he hiked up his book bag higher on his shoulder.

As he got into the building, Josh turned to me, "We're finally free!"

I swatted him on the arm but laughed. I knew he was kidding.

"I know you wore those sunglasses so no one would see you crying," Josh teased.

"Shut up. I did not," I protested.

I totally did. He knew me so well.

"Let's get home. I need to work."

I walked beside him to the car and he reached out and grasped my fingers in his. *He* still liked holding my hand in public.

When Josh is in town he works out of our house. I love the arrangement. It allows for some flexibility when he is home. For instance, if the kids have a function that fits, he'll go over his lunch hour and spend it with them. I love that. And I think he does, too.

We drove home and he was already taking a call before we got in the house. I walked in and plopped down on the couch. Molly climbed into my lap.

Before I could even flinch, she licked me on the nose. "OK," I said. "I get it. Your turn."

NINE

Kenpo's killer workouts

August 2013

I HAD BEEN home with my kids for 10 years now and that was really all I knew. I had my writing to keep me busy, but I needed something more since I couldn't do that all day while the kids were at school. I had published my second book, *Hiding in Plain Sight*, in April and my next book, *Spitfire*, would be out in a couple of months. But I needed to get healthy. Maybe if I started working out I would feel better.

Josh had left on a business trip and called me one night a few days into the first week of school. We talk every night when he's on the road. He always calls me at 10 p.m. and we normally talk about 30 minutes. That's one thing I love about our relationship: how we communicate. I tell him everything.

"Hey, babe! How was your day?" he asked. This is how every single one of our conversations starts.

"Good. How was yours?" I asked him.

"You tell me about yours first. How is school going for the kids?"

"They all really like it I think, although Carter says his teacher is mean and yells a lot."

"Oh, poor Carter man," Josh said on the other end of the line.

"He'll be fine. He always makes the best out of every situation. Hey, I'm totally switching topics here, but do you mind if I join this gym called Orange Theory Fitness?" We always talk to the other spouse if the thing we're buying is over $250.

"What is it?"

"I went and checked it out with Denise and it looks cool. They have rowers, treadmills, and a weight section. I guess you wear a heart monitor to see what your heart rate is. You want to be some in the green, some in the orange, and a little in the red. They have trainers that pump music and tell you what to do," I explained.

"That sounds cool. Sure, why don't you go for it?"

"OK good, I'm glad you said that. I already signed up for the free week. I start tomorrow," I laughed.

I could hear Josh chuckling on the other end, "Of course you did, Katers."

"What? I still talked to you about it."

"True. No, I think it'll be fun for you to get out and start an exercise program for once in your life."

"That's real nice. I played volleyball in high school," I argued.

"Riding the pine doesn't count," he teased.

"Hey now, I once aced an entire game, I'll have you know. We won that game. I swear people were chanting "Kate, Kate" just like they did in the movie *Rudy*."

"Oh, it's getting deep now."

"Just ask any of my high school friends like Angie or Jordan— on second thought don't ask them." Those girls and I had a running joke because I would tell jokes or stories on the bench and whenever the coach leaned forward to tell me to go in, I would lean back so he couldn't see me. I think I was the only person who got more of a workout from running my mouth than actually playing volleyball.

"Uh-huh. Then I'm sorry that I'm not sorry that I said that," I could tell he was smiling when he said that.

I finished telling him about my day and the kids. He told me about his day but they almost always consisted of presentations, meetings, dinners, and working on e-mails till one o'clock in the morning. He worked hard when he was on the road, putting in 16-17 hours in a day. Josh was always exhausted when he got home from his trips.

I shut off the TV and checked on the kids before turning off the lights. I let Molly out for a few minutes and decided it was time for bed. I'm a night owl and often stay up till 11 or 11:30 p.m. during the week.

I washed my face and brushed my teeth. I collapsed into my bed and Molly curled up next to me.

I DROPPED THE kids off at school and then raced home. I only had a few minutes to throw in a load of laundry before I was going to Orange Theory, or OTF as most people called it. I had talked my neighbor, Denise, into going with me. I was picking her up for the 9:15 a.m. class.

I grabbed my water bottle and tied up my shoes. As I clapped my hands together, Molly jumped and seemed scared.

"Oh, sorry girl. I'm just pumped to go to OTF," I said bending to pet her head.

Setting my home alarm, I opened the garage and whipped open my car door as the heavy wooden door started to slowly lift. I climbed in my car and cranked the engine. Throwing the car into reverse I quickly backed it up. When Josh was out of town, I parked smack in the middle of the garage. No need to take out my side mirrors on the garage, not that I've ever done that before.

As I drove the few houses down to pick up Denise, I clicked on the radio and found an upbeat song. Denise was waiting in the driveway. She smiled as she walked in front of the car and climbed in the front seat.

"Hey, girl. You ready?" I asked.

"Let's do this!"

Denise was already in great shape I thought. She told me that she had no muscle tone but used to be a runner.

We pulled up to OTF and I got a little nervous feeling in the pit of my stomach. I was a little like Carter and Chase when I was trying something new.

I grabbed my water bottle and pushed the key fob locking the doors to my car. We walked briskly into the building, as we had to fill out some paperwork before they would let us work out. I guess to protect them in case we got hurt or worse—died. I wasn't confident that I wouldn't do the first one.

We got fitted for our bands that wrapped around our torsos and were instructed to add a "pod" to it. This number would tell the front desk girls which of us had the pod so they could display our name on the monitor.

I walked into the large room and decided I was going to start on the rowers. The choice was to start either on the rowers, treadmills, or weight room. We wouldn't stay at one station for more than a few minutes before we were switching it up.

The class had a few minutes before it started so a trainer, S, was showing me how to use the treadmills to optimize my performance. He was a nice guy and I found that I continued to bob my head up and down a lot.

I told Denise that I was going to start on the rower and she decided to as well. We both climbed on. They were positioned in a line and I looked up at the monitor and saw my name. I was in the blue zone. That couldn't be good. I guessed that my heart rate was at rest.

I put my feet in the stirrups and pulled back on the handles. I immediately felt the pull in my back.

"Damn, what did we get ourselves into?" I looked over at Denise and smiled.

This was way different than volleyball.

"Hey, I like your Adidas shirt," a woman on my left said.

I turned toward her and replied, "I got it at Kohl's. They were having a sale and I got some Kohl's bucks to go with it."

She smiled. "Gotta love Kohl's. I'll have to check it out."

"I'm Kate, by the way. Today is my first day."

"I'm Alexa. You're going to love it. I've been coming for about six months and could tell a difference after about three months."

"Really? I want arms that look like yours." I looked over at her toned arms and tried to hide my chicken fat that seemed to shake every time I pulled the handles back on the rower.

Running on the treadmill in front of me was this woman with coal black hair. Her arms were slim and toned and her butt looked tight and firm. Yes, I can appreciate beauty in any form.

"I want to look like her," I said to Alexa.

"That's Tanya, and so do I," Alexa said and laughed.

"OK, people! Let's get this class started!" S said over his headset. The music started pumping.

I glanced up at the monitor and noticed I was already in the green.

Well, would you look at that? My heart actually beats harder when I push it.

The clock was counting down the time and we began by doing all-outs or "base" on each of the rowers and treadmills. The weight room portion killed me. Seriously, how could 5 pounds be so heavy? Thank goodness I signed that waiver.

I successfully finished the class and had burned 518 calories.

"That was awesome! What did you think?" I asked Denise on the way to the car.

"Yeah, I liked it, too. I think we should sign up."

"Alright. Let's get our free week first and then join after that. I think there's a special going on right now."

THIS IS HOW the next few months of my days would go. I joined the unlimited membership and started going six days a week. And that's when I met Kenpo. I soon found out that Kenpo wasn't his real name. All of the trainers had stage names. Every time I heard that, all I could think of was strippers.

I once asked him about his stripper name—I mean his stage name. He told me that he was a black belt in karate and people would call him Kenpo because he knocked people out.

Over the next few months, he totally knocked me out and kicked my butt in the process. I started going to most of his classes because that's when Tanya and Alexa would go. I looked forward to seeing them and having a little social time before and after class.

Today I had a little time before the class started and I was adjusting my pod.

"Hey, girl. How are you?" Tanya asked as she swung open the door.

That chick made yoga pants and workout clothes look fabulous. I hated her.

"Hey! Are we ready for this?" I asked and then sighed. I was still sore from the beating Kenpo gave me yesterday.

She took a sip of her protein shake and threw her keys in the cubby next to the bathroom.

"Absolutely. What are you starting on?"

"I think I'll do the rowers. I like to warm up on them. Where are you starting?"

"The treadmill for sure. I can't seem to get my heart rate up otherwise. Have you seen Alexa lately?"

No sooner had Tanya spoken those words than Alexa came rushing through the door.

"Hey, ladies! Whew! Busy morning with work. Are there any pods left?" she asked the front desk girls.

V handed her the number nine pod. She took it and snapped it into place.

"You starting on the rowers?"

"Yep. Are you?" I asked her.

"Yes, let's see if we can get two together." I followed her into the work out room and it was still pretty steamy from the class before us. The music was already on but at a low level.

We found two rowers near the front of the row and I plopped down and set my water bottle next to me.

"Hey, ladies! Are you ready to work?" Kenpo came over to where we had already started to warm up.

I looked up at the man in front of me. He always wore an orange tank top and his arms looked like he had blown them up. He was chiseled and I quietly hated the excellent shape he was in.

"I'm only ready if you promise not to do legs again. Seriously, I couldn't even sit on the toilet without screaming in pain. I was cussing you every time I sat down," I accused him.

"You're such a wuss. I think I'll do more legs just for you," he smiled and rubbed his hand over his black goatee.

"You suck," I rolled my eyes at him.

"Row faster," he spun his finger in a circle, "this isn't blue theory. Get into the orange!"

I adjusted my gloves and snapped the Velcro tighter in place. I started to pull back faster and harder on the handles.

"Thank goodness for these gloves. I was starting to get callouses," I said over my shoulder to Alexa, "No one wants man hands!"

She laughed and set her face into serious mode getting ready to work.

"Alright! Move it. Ya, buddy!" Kenpo clicked on his infamous song *Let's Go* that he started every class with. I smiled and started to stand back further in the stirrups until I felt the burn in my calves.

Kenpo started pushing us through his torturous exercises. I glanced up at the monitor and noticed I was sitting steady in the green.

"Orange, girl. You need more orange," Kenpo leaned down and "encouraged" me.

"Go pick on someone else... someone not as awesome as me," I grunted back at him while the muscles in my back groaned.

Kenpo laughed and then spoke on his mic, "Listen up. Time to tornado! Switch!"

People started to climb off of the rowers and I moved slowly to a standing position.

"Move it, sister!" Kenpo hollered in my ear. He held out his fist and I bumped it on the way by.

"He's lucky I didn't just punch him in the face instead!" I half shouted over the music to Tanya as I moved to the weight room.

She grinned and her dark ponytail bobbed up and down and she went and collected a set of 25 pound weights for her set in the weight room.

"Oh, hell no," I muttered looking down at her weights and then picked up 10 pound weights for me instead.

"Watch me for this round of exercises and then it's all you for three sets," Kenpo explained and I watched as he effortlessly showed the squats and other forms of torture that were supposed to make me stronger if it didn't kill me first.

Sweat dripped down my brow and I wiped it away quickly with my orange towel. My breathing was already labored and we were only 33 minutes in.

I purposely picked a location in the back so I could focus on what I was doing. Plus, I didn't want people to see how horribly uncoordinated I was.

Kenpo's music was pumping and I started to move my hips around and bop my head to the beat. I lip synced the next phrase of the song to Denise and laughed as she joined my dance party in the back.

We were supposed to be jumping up on a riser and then off. I was getting tired just watching the other people doing it.

"I don't think sooooo…" I sang out the last word to Denise and shook my thumb over my shoulder at the riser. "That's a good way for me to fall on my ass."

I laughed as I watched Denise do her own version of the exercise. I was still chuckling when I noticed Kenpo coming around the corner.

"Oh, shit. What were we supposed to be doing?" I quickly grabbed my weights and began to pump them.

"Nah, those are no good," Kenpo grabbed my 10-pound weights from me and replaced them with 20-pound ones. "Do the kettle bells with these. Challenge yourself, wussy."

"Excuse me. I was perfectly fine being unchallenged over here in my little corner. Go ruin someone else's workout," I waved my hand at Kenpo, dismissing him.

Kenpo feigned being shocked and laughed. He was already moving on to Denise.

"Watch out, Dee! You're about to get more weight!" I shouted over the music to Denise. She just continued to do her own thing and stared down Kenpo. He started to walk toward her and then moved away after he caught her steady glance.

That chick has steel balls.

I shook my head and chuckled. Kenpo later told me that Denise intimidated him.

"Ya, buddy! Ok, good work everybody. Let's stretch it out and I'm going to fill you in on my next challenge," Kenpo turned down the music and everyone moved from their stations closer to where he was standing.

He placed his right arm across his chest. "Stretch it out for a hold of 10. My next challenge is one where you'll pick teams of three. There will be a new challenge every week and the team with the most points for that week will move on. I'll explain each week how you can get more points. The winning teams will go to the Super Bowl and can win prizes like a new pair of custom made shoes from Nike." He switched arms and leaned into another stretch.

"You need to come up with a team name and let me know the members of your team by Friday if you want to participate. Don't forget to drink your water and get all your protein in today. See you next time!"

People began filing out of the room and high-fiving Kenpo as they walked past him.

I squatted down to stretch my legs out and then slumped down on the floor until I was lying flat on my back. The coolness of the tile washed over me.

"Damn, that feels good," I closed my eyes and could almost feel every one of my muscles already screaming in pain.

"Nice work today, girl," Alexa was standing above me. "You burned 538 calories."

"Yeah, but look at my pyramid. That's a lot of red. I don't think I'm supposed to have that much but I couldn't seem to get out of it today."

"I don't know how you burn so many calories. I only burned 495," Alexa stated and wiped her towel across her face.

"Only isn't really the right word that goes with 495 calories. Do you know how much cake you can now eat? I think you did a great job! What is it about Kenpo and his ass-whipping classes? Seriously, I'm so sore every morning I wake up. A small tear rolls down my face even when I'm brushing my teeth."

Alexa laughed, "I know what you mean. Hey, do you want to be on a team together?"

"I'd love that! Who should we get for a third person?" I asked.

"I was thinking maybe Tanya? I think she's still out in the lobby. Should we go ask her?"

"That would be a good team. Yeah, let's go ask her—can you carry me out there?" I groaned and then grinned up at her.

Alexa reached out her hand to me to help me up.

"No, seriously? I don't think I can walk..." I grimaced as I stood up.

She smiled and pulled me up by the arm, "Come on, girl!"

"The floor was so comfy, though!" I could see Tanya leaving through the front door as we were making our way to the lobby.

"Hey, T, wait up!" I hollered at her.

Tanya was pulling her hair tie out of her hair and ran her fingers through her wet strands.

"Hey girlies. What's up?"

"Do you think you'll do Kenpo's challenge?" Alexa asked.

"I think so. Sounds like it'll be fun!"

"Do you want to be on our team?" I asked Tanya, motioning with my finger between Alexa and me.

"Oh, yeah! That sounds like a lot of fun! Kenpo said we have to come up with a team name. I can e-mail him and let him know that we're going to be doing the challenge together. What should our name be?"

Alexa glanced down at her watch, "Hey, girls, I have to scoot to work. Let's text later and come up with a name. Have a good afternoon!" She tossed her pod into the small container on the way out the door.

"Sounds good. See ya, Alexa!" I smiled, waved at her and then turned to Tanya. "Damn, even waving hurts my less-than-toned arms. You sure you want to be on a team with someone that can't even wave without injuring herself?"

"I'm sure," Tanya grinned and wrapped her arm around my shoulder. She gave me a squeeze and then walked next to me out to the parking lot.

"What should we have our name be?"

"Hmm. I was thinking maybe like Kenpo's babes? Or no, how about Kenpo's Angels?" I said.

"That could be cute—like Charlie's Angels? I'm thinking we need shirts or something."

"I'll let you work on that one. Let's text Alexa and see what she thinks about the team name."

"Are you free this week if we work on doing some shirts? I was thinking we could get some cheap tanks or something."

"This week is crazy for me. Josh is out of town Monday to Thursday and I have to run the kids to their activities every night. I might be able to meet up with you girls later on? Can I let you know?"

"Sure, no problem. I'll text Alexa and see if she could bring over her little guy and he can play with my G while we knock out some shirts. What do you want yours to say?"

"My shirt?" I asked her. I chewed my bottom lip and thought for a second.

Tanya nodded and smiled.

"I want it to say just one word—Badass."

Tanya looked and me to see if I was being serious.

I smiled big and nodded once. "Yep. Badass. Because I'm one badass angel."

Little did I know that I would need that confident attitude in the next couple of months. And my strength... not only the strength that I gained from Kenpo's classes, but also from the other "angels" I had in my life.

TEN

Buddy

PUSHING MY TARGET cart down one aisle, I paused and started looking at the Lego sets. I propped my right foot up on the edge of the cart and leaned over so my arms were bent in front of me on the handle. I dropped my face into my hand and blew out a sigh. I don't know why I was so tired but this daily headache was getting old.

I went to bed with a headache and woke up with one. Every day, it was still there—some days a migraine and others a dull ache. Randy helped me to get some relief in physical therapy, but I was ready to not have this pounding in my head.

"You have two of them? OK, great! We'll be in shortly to look at them," Josh's voice got louder as he got excited about something, and I heard his footsteps coming closer to where I was standing.

He stopped when he got to my aisle and quickly slipped his phone in his pocket.

"You'll never guess what I just found..." he grinned slyly.

Josh and I were birthday shopping for Carter's upcoming birthday. On Fridays if Josh is home from traveling, we do a lunch date. We always do the kids' birthday and Christmas shopping together and were picking up a few things for Carter's birthday that weekend.

"You found us two new iPhones?" We wanted to update to the iPhone 5 but were having trouble finding them in the stores.

"Nope, even better."

"What can be better?"

"A Goldendoodle puppy."

"What did you do?" I asked him hesitantly.

"Well, you know how hard it is to find Goldendoodles? I called the pet shop and they have two boy puppies in. I told them we would come look at them. Carter wants another puppy."

"He does, huh? Are you sure you don't want another puppy?"

"Maybe," he answered in a singsong voice.

"I'm the one that will end up doing all the work, like walking him and feeding and well, everything."

"Probably, but you're so good at it."

I swatted his arm as we walked toward the door.

"OK, let's go look at your new puppy... I mean Carter's new puppy," I winked at him.

"He'll be so excited!"

"Uh-huh. He will be." I shook my head and followed Josh out the door.

WE PICKED UP the kids from school and took them immediately to the pet shop. I would love to go to the rescue to buy my dogs, but my kids are really allergic to most dogs. Carter has ended up in the emergency room after spending time with my brother-in-law's

Pekinese dogs. He can't breathe and goes into an asthma attack. We have to get dogs that are a mix with a poodle so they don't shed as much. We always "try out" different dogs to see how he'll do reacting to them.

"How was everyone's day?" I asked as the kids piled in the car.

Chase and Jillian started talking at the same time. Carter just smiled and said, "Fine."

I looked over at Josh and grinned. I loved how all of our kids had the talking gene like me. Josh is a very quiet man once you get to know him. He was described as a powerful introvert by our pastor once and it fit him perfectly.

"Where are we going?" Chase asked as we drove past the entrance to our neighborhood.

"We're going to look at Goldendoodles for Carter's birthday!" Josh was practically squealing with delight.

"Or for Dad…" I mumbled under my breath.

"Catherine… I heard that." Josh calls me Catherine when he's trying to scold me for something. I ignore it mostly.

"We get to try out a Goldendoodle? I want one!" Jillian has now jumped on the new-dog bandwagon.

"We'll see… we have to see how Carter does. Let's go look at them and then make a family decision."

"It'll be like the time when I was 4 and we got Molly for my birthday. Do you remember that, Mom?" Carter asked.

I laughed, "Of course I do! You were the cutest thing. I pulled up to your preschool and I had Molly on my lap. You got so excited that you yelled out to your friends that you had gotten a puppy for your birthday." I grinned over at Josh and saw that he was smiling, too. Carter had heard that story a hundred times but still liked for me to tell it.

"Really? Carter gets to have two dogs?" Chase asked.

"Yes, because Carter is the favorite. Deal with it," Josh teased and looked up into the rearview mirror at Chase.

"You stink, Dad. It's not fair. Carter is already Molly's favorite."

"It'll be a family dog just like Molly is. Everyone will have to help take care of him. Everyone," I said. I looked at Josh and cleared my throat.

"That's right kids, listen to your mother. You all will have to clean up after the dogs and walk them," Josh explained, pulling into a parking space.

"I wasn't talking about just them..." I winked at Josh and opened my door to get out.

"Slow down! Hang on. Hold my hand," I scolded Jillian as she darted off toward the store.

Josh held the door open for us and I shook my head at him in response to the goofy grin he had on his face.

"What're you getting us into?"

"You love it," he swatted my rear end as I passed through the door. It was easy to hear my kids had already found the puppies. I chuckled as we walked back to where the kids were cooing to the puppies and tapping on the glass.

A salesperson came up and smiled at my kids. "Can I get one out for you to play with?"

"We would love that. Thank you," Josh beamed and questioned, "Which one?"

I looked at the two brothers and pointed, "The one on the left, please."

"He *is* cuter, Mom," Carter said. He smiled and slipped his hand in mine as we walked to the viewing room.

There was one chair in the room, but otherwise it was small and bare.

"Let Mom have the chair," Josh squeezed my shoulder as I sat down. He could tell when I was hurting even though I would always tell him I was fine.

The puppy climbed all over the kids and licked their faces. Their sweet laughter filled the small room and I inhaled deeply. I knew that I would remember this moment for a long time.

"What should we call him? I mean, if we end up getting him?"

"How about Bruno or Brownie..."

"How about Buddy..." All of the kids were shouting out names at once.

"He does look like a Buddy. I like it. Carter, how are you feeling bud? Any reactions?" I asked.

"Nope. I'm good. Can we get him?"

"Yeah, can we get him, Mom?" Josh looked down at me and had a huge grin on his face.

"How can I say no to this face?" I rubbed my hands over Buddy's soft fur on his head and smiled. "Welcome to the family, Buddy."

HE WASN'T OLD enough to go home with us that day. When we went back to pick him up, Buddy had grown. I'm not talking a few pounds—I'm talking like 15 pounds.

Josh carried him like a baby out of the store.

As he walked through the door, a woman asked, "Is that a Goldendoodle?"

"It sure is," Josh replied.

"I wasn't sure. It's hard to remember when ours was ever that small..."

When she walked away, I swallowed.

"That small? What the heck? He's huge!" I said to Josh.

He just shrugged and pretended like the small pony he was carrying in his arms wasn't heavy.

"He'll be fine. I doubt he'll get much bigger."

The lady in the store told us that Buddy would probably get around 55 pounds. He currently weighed 35 pounds and seemed huge compared to Molly's 12-pound frame.

We got him into the house and Molly seemed irritated that we brought this giant fur ball home. She's the alpha and even now continues to boss him around.

We took him right outside to show him the yard.

"Set him down, Dad," Jillian instructed.

I watched as Buddy took a few lone steps and headed straight toward our pool.

"Watch him! He's going to fall in," I warned.

"He's fine. Let's just see what he does."

I watched with a nervous eye as the dopey puppy took another step and fell head first into the pool onto the 3-foot deep shelf.

"Grab him, Dad!" Chase yelled.

"Get him, babe!" I yelled at the same time.

Josh fished him out and Buddy shook himself off and then frolicked over to the grassy area. He wasn't bothered one bit.

"Buddy's going to fit into our family just fine," Josh volunteered.

"I know what you're thinking," I said.

"What am I thinking?"

"That he doesn't have any athletic skills apparently, either."

Josh laughed, "Maybe."

ELEVEN
Pimp Limp

MY ALARM STARTED beeping at 4:45 a.m.. I sighed and threw the covers off me.

"What the hell is that noise?" Josh grumbled. He flexed his fingers that he had on my hip. His warmth was radiating next to me.

"Shh. Go back to sleep. I'm doing doubles today at Orange."

"Are you nuts? You about killed yourself last week doing doubles. You're doing too much. You're going to hurt yourself," Josh followed me into the bathroom and squinted when I switched on the light.

"Damn, that's bright. Sorry, babe," I flipped the overhead one off and turned on the closet light. I slipped my angel tank over my sports bra and grabbed my shorts off the shelf.

Josh flushed the toilet and was washing his hands. I could feel him watching me in the mirror.

I winced as I pulled my shorts up over my hips. My left hamstring was already starting to complain from the overuse.

"I saw that. Seriously, Kater, you need to be done," he dried his hands and looked at me.

"I know and I will be... soon. We are in the finals and are so close to winning this whole thing. You know that I've never had too much success in the athletic world, so it feels good to have gone so far. And I can't let down Tanya and Alexa," I bent to pull on my shoes and took a quick bite out of my power bar. "Today's challenge is the most calories burned—the girls need me. The second class is a perfect pyramid so I can go easy on that one."

Josh shook his head. "I just worry about you, that's all."

"I know you do. I'll be fine. Promise. Go back to bed. I'll be home to get the kids to school." I gave him a quick peck on the lips and grabbed my orange towel on the way out of my bedroom.

I tiptoed to the kitchen and quietly opened the refrigerator to get my energy drink. The dim light threw a shadow on the kitchen floor. I glanced at the time on the microwave and saw that I needed to get a move on.

I scooped up my keys and headed toward the garage. I opened the car door and slid inside, breaking open my drink while I waited for the heavy wooden garage door to open.

The cold liquid tasted too sugary that early in the morning. I never drank energy drinks and only did so now so I could rev up my heart rate. When I worked out, it always pushed me and kept me in the red. I could burn 750 calories an hour and knew that my team needed the extra points.

I rubbed my eyes as I sat at the stop light. I was tired and sore. My body was starting to shut down from all the overuse. I reached over and rubbed my shoulder with my right hand. I could feel the muscle under my palm and it was tight.

In the last three months, I had gained more muscle in my body than I've ever had in my life. I went from weighing 133 pounds to 144 pounds. I'm 5'9" and I remember crying to Josh once about the extra weight I had put on.

"Do you want to be strong or skinny fat?" Josh had asked.

"I want to be skinny *and* muscular." I wiped away a small tear.

Josh chuckled, "It doesn't work that way. If you don't like how you look with muscle, just stop working out and you'll lose it pretty fast."

I blinked and stared at him.

"I like how I feel when I'm strong."

"OK. Well then, there's your answer..."

The stoplight changed and my foot switched from the brake to the gas. I was going to get through this challenge and then I had to stop this seven-days-a-week workout plan I had been doing.

I needed a break. My body needed a break.

I whipped into the parking lot and saw the other early bird workout people heading into Orange Theory. I switched off the ignition and jumped out of the car.

The morning was a bit chilly as I walked to the building. I knew that I would be warmed up in no time.

"What's up my angels?" I pulled open the door and smiled as I saw Tanya pulling her ponytail tighter. She was wearing her tank that she and Alexa had decorated. Hers said "Power" on it. She couldn't think of what to put on her tank, but "Power" fit. She was a powerhouse. Alexa had chosen "OCD". It fit her perfectly and always made me smile when we had our tanks on. The girls had used rhinestones to put "Badass", "OCD", and "Power" on the front. The backs had angel wings that were spread to look like they were flying.

"Morning, girl. We need to make sure to remind Kenpo that we wore our team shirts so we can get more points today," Tanya pulled her tank down over her hips.

"OK, I'll put it in my e-mail to him. Is Alexa here?" I looked around the lobby for our friend.

A quiet knock could be heard on the window that separated the lobby from the workout area.

Alexa knocked and waved at us, standing over a rower. She motioned for us to come in.

"Good Lord... it's early. I'm already tired and we haven't even started," I grumbled out as we walked over to where Alexa was standing.

"How do you do it?" I asked Alexa.

"Do what?" she asked, quizzedly.

"Look so good and well rested at the butt crack of dawn," I responded to Alexa, with her fresh, no makeup face.

Alexa laughed, "I did go to bed at 8:30 p.m. last night soooo..."

"Whatever. You always look like this. It's seriously not fair to the rest of us," I climbed onto the rower and strapped my feet in. "You starting on the treadmill, T?"

"You know it, sista," Tanya walked away and stepped up on the treadmill.

I saw Kenpo out of the corner of my eye. He put on the headset and flipped on the music. *Let's Go* started pumping through the speakers.

"Kill me now," I muttered under my breath and pulled back on the handles, feeling the burn.

I was tired this morning so I wasn't having my normal dance party in the back or talking much. I was concentrating on keeping my heart rate up so I could stay in the red and burn more calories. And it was too damned early for me to have much energy, anyway.

"What's up this morning? Way to get after your weights, girl," Kenpo slapped me on the back as he walked by me in the weight room.

I smiled up at him as I bent over to grab my now 15-pound weights in each hand. I was about halfway through my set of 10, climbing up and over the riser with the weights in my hand.

Pain sheared down from my left hip and hamstring.

Shit! What was that?

My weights dropped to the floor and I grabbed the small space where my quad met my hip. I grabbed my foot and tried to stretch out my hamstring. It felt bunched up and I couldn't get it to release no matter what I did.

I glanced up at the clock. Four minutes to go.

I can do this.

Sweat dripped down from my face and fell to the floor. I bent and picked up my weights and just started pumping them. I needed to get the last few calories I could so I could get seven points. I was only eight calories away from 700 and I was going to get to seven hundred today—injured or not.

"Ya, buddy! All right, everybody. That's class. Please pick up your weights and equipment at your stations and come over to stretch," Kenpo passed out some cleaning wipes to the people on the treadmills.

I looked up at the monitor and saw that I had burned 712 calories. I took my weights over to the rack and found as soon as I put any weight on my leg that I had immediate pain. I limped over to where Tanya and Alexa were stretching.

"Uh-oh. What happened? Why are you limping?" Tanya asked with one eyebrow cocked.

"I think I pulled something. I have a burning pain right here," I rubbed my fingers into my hip tendon.

Alexa sat on the floor with her right leg in front of her. "I think you need to stretch more, Kate. Sit down," she patted the floor with her hand.

I sat down and winced, as the pain seemed to get worse every time I moved.

Kenpo walked over to where we were stretching. "Nice work today, angels. You killed it on calories today, Kate," he smiled and held up his hand for me to slap it.

"Yeah, but not as much as normal. I seriously think I hurt myself. I heard a popping noise or something and have so much pain going down my leg."

"Try icing when you get home and use some Icy Hot on it."

"OK, I'll get some on the way home. Hey, help me up, would ya?"

He grabbed my wrists and pulled me to my feet.

"See ya, girls. I'm off to go ice. Don't be jealous of my pimp limp!" I called over my shoulder, smiling at them.

"Text us later!" Tanya shouted back.

I STOPPED AT the store on my way home and was applying the Icy Hot on my entire left side. I was slathering my hip with the gel-like stuff and felt a puffy bulge.

"What the heck is that?" I questioned myself and looked closer at it in the mirror.

I had been lifting more weight lately. Maybe I had gotten a hernia. Flipping on the water, I quickly washed off my hands before I grabbed my phone.

I punched in a quick text to Kris.

Me: *Hey, think I may have a hernia. Can you look at it pls when you get home?*

Kris: *Sure. I'm home. I'll come over.*

Luckily for me, Kris is a colon rectal surgeon and an awesome guy. While I waited for him to come over, I screwed on the cap and put the tube away in the drawer. I could already feel the cool sensation spreading over my hip.

The doorbell rang and the dogs went nuts barking. We have a locked front gate so I went through the garage and opened the door.

"Hey, Kris! Thanks for taking a look at me."

"It's no problem. Did you do this working out?"

"Yep. Orange Theory," I led him through the hallway into the family room.

"I thought you were going to slow down a little bit on the workouts?"

Kris and Shayla knew about how crazy I had been working out lately.

"I am—just as soon as I finish this challenge," I pulled down the left side of my pants. The bulge was low, really low, and I looked down into the cute face of my friend as he knelt in front of me.

"Um... so, do you..." Kris rambled out.

"Just do it! Go ahead and check. It's fine," my face got warm and I died a little on the inside. He was a doctor for goodness sake but it didn't help that my attractive friend had to feel my lower hip area. My girlfriends had all seen Kris and one once told me that he could do an exam on her anytime. For me—not so much. Kris and Shayla were our really good friends and we travel with them sometimes.

He pressed very gently and went into professional mode while checking me for a hernia. As he pushed he was explaining to me that it could be a femoral hernia, which occurs when a part of the intestine bulges near the groin and thigh.

"I don't think it's a hernia but there's only one accurate way to be sure," Kris explained standing up.

"How do you know for sure?"

"Well, you know that when checking men, doctors feel and press in their testicles?"

"You mean like the turn and cough thing?"

"Yes. But for women, you have to feel their labia—"

"OK, stop right there. Some things can't be unseen..." I made a goofy grin over at my friend. "I guess I'll call and make an appointment with my doctor."

"Good idea. And Kate: Seriously, you need to stop working out for a bit to let your body heal."

"I know I do, but it's just that this challenge is almost done. Then I'll stop. Promise."

"If it were me or Shayla, I'd be done." He walked toward the garage door. "It's not like you can't work out again later, but just give it a rest for a while."

I nodded and smiled, "Thanks for checking me. Nando's this weekend?"

About once a week or every other, we go to this Mexican restaurant as a family with Kris and Shayla and their kids. We all order the same thing. They are busy a lot and it's hard to mesh our schedules sometimes, but if I really want to make sure they'll go out with us, I always suggest Nando's. It's a given that they'll go.

"Yes, that'll work. How about Saturday at 5:30 p.m.?"

"Done. Thanks again. Have a good night," I opened the door for him and watched him leave my garage before punching the button to close the door.

"See ya!" Kris waved over his shoulder as the garage door slowly closed behind him.

I WENT TO my doctor and after she examined me, she determined that I needed to have a pelvic CT scan to see if I had a hernia or not. And no, she didn't do "the test" as Kris suggested may need to be done. I asked her to skip that since we were doing the CT. Thankfully, she obliged.

While waiting on the results of my CT, I was forced to stop working out. My entire left leg was now numb down to my foot. I would get sharp pains and pins and needles in my heel. Also, I was having a hard time going to the bathroom because I couldn't feel anything from the waist down.

Since I hadn't worked out in a few weeks, my muscle was quickly deteriorating. All of the muscle that I had worked so hard to build was nearly gone and I was losing weight. At first it was just a few pounds, but after almost a month of not being active, I was back down to 134 pounds.

The dryer timer went off and I padded slowly into the laundry room to get the clothes out. I didn't have much energy and seemed to do everything in slow motion.

I swung open the door and leaned down to get the clothes out. My cell phone rang in my pocket.

"Hello?" I asked.

"Hello, may I please speak to Catherine Mathias?"

"This is she."

"Catherine, we have the results of your CT. Can you come in today to discuss them?"

Here we go again.

"You can't give them to me over the phone?"

"I'm afraid not. I do have a 1:30 p.m. time slot open. Does that work for you?"

"Sure, I'll be there. Thank you."

I clicked the phone off and then quickly thumbed a text

off to Josh.

Me: *I'm going in at 1:30 for the results of my CT. Why do they always make me come in?*

Josh: *It's just normal procedure. Don't be worried. Call me when ur done. Luv u!*

Me: *Ok. Luv u!*

Glancing at the time before I locked my phone, I realized I only had about 30 minutes before I needed to leave. I scooped out the clothes and threw them on my bed. I would have to sort them later.

FEELINGS OF BEING here before filled me with dread as I sat on the small exam table waiting for the door to open and Dr. L to come in. It had only been a year since I was diagnosed with the stroke.

The wooden door swung open and Dr. L walked through with a smile on her face.

"How are you doing, Kate?"

"Hi, Dr. L. I'm hanging in there. I now have pain and numbness down my left leg. Do I have a hernia?"

I watched as Dr. L bent to sit down.

Don't sit on the stool. Don't sit on the stool.

Cringing as she sat and wheeled closer to me, a sickening feeling filled my stomach.

She patted the chair next to her, "Why don't you move to this chair and we can go over these results?"

I did as she asked and tried to steal a glance at what the results may say.

"First off, no hernia."

"Well, that's good news," I sighed and smiled at her. Maybe I was worrying for nothing.

"However, they did find a little something on the scan."

I swallowed hard and leaned closer to her. The two sheets of paper rustled in her hands and my eyes immediately started scanning the dark words.

"It appears as though you have some thickening on your bladder... and we need to check..."

Her words became mute in my mind as my eyes caught the word carcinoma.

Cancer?

"I'm sorry. What were you saying? Why do I see the word, carcinoma? Do I have bladder cancer?" The words tumbled out of my mouth and my hand immediately went to my throat, shaky and clammy.

"That is a possibility. I'm going to refer you to a urologist to have this further evaluated," she said. Her eyes got large as she looked at me. "Take the next 10 seconds to have a freak out and then you have to let it go." Her hand dropped to my leg that was bouncing on the floor.

My eyes brimmed with tears and dryness filled my mouth.

"Not again. I can't have something wrong with me again. I have three kids... my husband is gone all the time. I can't. Just can't," as the words stumbled out of me she reached over and pulled a few tissues from the box.

"I know, honey. I know what you've already been through. Here's the deal though. You're not going to Google this on the Internet and go home all worried about it. You have to stay strong for your kids until you have a chance to meet with the urologist."

"OK, I won't look it up," I gulped.

As soon as she leaves, I'm totally looking it up.

"What else can I do for you in the meantime? What about your leg pain?"

My left hand automatically went to my left thigh and I rubbed my palm down it.

"Yeah, I have a lot of pain and can't really feel anything from the waist down. It's been hard to urinate or poop, too," I half whispered because my mind was still focused on seeing bladder cancer on that report.

"I'm going to prescribe some steroids to help bring the inflammation down. You must have some nerve damage from pulling that tendon. The steroids should help," she tore off the prescription from her pad and handed it to me.

"Thank you."

"Anything I can do to help in the meantime, you let me know. My nurse will bring in a name of a urologist so you can make an appointment."

"OK, thank you Dr. L."

She nodded, "Be well."

I blindly left the office and couldn't believe that I was facing another health problem. Why was this happening to me?

As I drove toward the pharmacy, I called Josh. While I waited for him to answer, I looked at the clock. He was probably still in the air. He wouldn't be available for another 30 minutes or so.

I clicked the phone off, as I wasn't going to leave a voicemail about this. The next call I made was to my mom.

She answered with her normal cheery voice, "Hi, honey!"

"Hey, Mom. I just finished at the doctor. Umm—"

"What is it, honey?"

"The doctor thinks I may have bladder cancer," I blurted out the words.

Mom gasped, "Oh, no! Why does she think that?"

"I guess I have thickening on my bladder. I have to go see a urologist to be looked at further. Mom? I can't do this again. I can't be sick..."

"I know Kater, as you've already been through so much. Dad just walked in. Let me put him on the line."

I could hear my mom's whisper as she quickly filled in my dad. He answered the phone and immediately his calm voice filled my ear.

"Hey, daughter. What's this I hear about bladder cancer?"

I tried to not sound blubbery but my words came out watery.

"Hi, Dad. My CT showed a thickening of my bladder wall. It said it was possibly bladder cancer."

"You aren't a typical candidate for bladder cancer."

"What do you mean?"

"Most people that get that are farmers or someone that holds their bladder for long periods of time. You don't really fit someone with the lifestyle. Are you going to see a urologist?"

"Yes, I have to make an appointment with one."

"OK, well, until we know for sure, let's not worry about the what-ifs."

"I know, Dad, but last time it really was something to worry about."

"I'm still not convinced that you had a stroke. You're a healthy, young woman that exercises often and takes care of herself. Let's just wait and see how this pans out before you get yourself all worked up."

"Too late for that."

Dad chuckled. "I know you're worried because you're a freak."

"Thanks for the vote of confidence," I smiled in spite of myself, silently thanking my dad for knowing how to lighten my mood.

"Anytime, honey. Now make that appointment and keep us posted. We love you."

"I love you guys, too. I'll let you know. Bye, Dad."

I pressed the disconnect button on my car to end the call and pulled into the drive-through lane at the pharmacy.

"Catherine Mathias to pick up medication, please."

"I see this is a new prescription. Would you like to talk to the pharmacist?"

"Sure. Thanks."

"Hi," the dark haired pharmacist addressed me while looking down at my medication, "This is a steroid pack. I wouldn't take this tonight, as it's too late in the afternoon. It'll keep you awake otherwise. Take the meds with some food as it can cause some stomach irritation. Do you have any questions?"

"No, I think I'm good. Thank you," I reached into the drawer and pulled out my medicine.

I drove home on autopilot and thankfully got there safely. I pulled into our driveway and opened the garage door. Josh's car was parked in his spot.

I pushed open the door and called out, "J? Are you home?"

"Hey! I'm in the bedroom."

I walked down the short hallway and smiled when I saw him.

"Hi," I reached up and wrapped my arms around his neck. "I missed you."

"I missed you. What did the doctor say?"

My eyes clouded up, "Hmm. Not too awesome of news. I may have bladder cancer."

"Seriously? Oh, babe. I know you must be scared," he wrapped his arm tighter on my waist. "We'll get through this just like we did the last time."

I looked up into his kind, blue eyes. "I'm tired of getting through things. Why do I keep having things happen to me?"

"I'm not sure. What can I do?" He leaned his head to the right and pinched his lips together.

"Take me out to dinner. I'm not cooking tonight. Not after finding out this news."

"Ha. That's not what I expected you to say, but sure, babe. Anything you want."

"Nando's?"

Josh grinned. "Nandos."

I LOOKED ACROSS the table at my three kids and smiled when I caught Josh's eye. Chase was telling a story about his day and it was helping me to forget about my latest health news.

"So my class was in the computer lab and this girl, S, and I printed our papers at the same time. We met in front of the printer and mine was on top of hers. She plucked off my paper and dropped it on the floor, stepping on it in the process," he paused and took a drink.

"She stepped on your paper? That wasn't very nice," I responded.

"Oh, just wait Mom, I got her back," he grinned slyly. "I bent over to pick up my paper and kinda scooted my booty toward her so it backed her up against the wall. Then I crop dusted her."

"Stop! You did not!" I laughed loudly and slapped my hand across my mouth.

Crop dusting is something that Josh's brother, Justin, taught the kids. It's when you pass gas silently and then leave when the smell is caught in the victim's face.

Chase nodded proudly, "Oh, yeah, it was awesome. I had school lunch's greasy cheeseburger so it smelled really horrible. It burned *my* eyes. I walked away with a smile on my face while she stood there and ate it."

"Oh, dear Lord," I muttered and then chuckled again.

We all laughed and it felt good to be surrounded by my family. The kids went back to coloring their menus and Josh reached over and squeezed my hand.

"How're you feeling, bear?"

"I'm OK."

"Liar."

I smiled weakly. He always knew when I was hiding how I felt.

"Why don't you go ahead and take the steroids? I think they will help."

"The pharmacist said not to this late as it'll keep me up."

"We're always up late though so I don't think it'll matter," Josh said.

I pulled the packet of steroids out of my purse and started popping the seven small pills into my hand.

"If you're sure?"

"Go for it! What can it hurt?" he asked.

IT CAN HURT a lot I found out later. I tossed and turned all night.

"Babe, what's wrong? What time is it?" Josh asked me sleepily.

"Two a.m. I don't know. I feel like my head is going to burst. I may need to go to the hospital. Seriously. Help me," I half whispered, half croaked, as I started to cry.

"Crying isn't going to help. C'mere," he pulled me closer to him and as my head drug across the pillow I let out a yelp. "It's that bad?"

"I've never been in so much pain my whole life. Can you get me some of my migraine medicine?"

"Sure. I'll be right back." Josh flipped the sheets off of him and got out of bed.

I could barely hear him, over the pounding in my head, rifling through my medicine cabinet looking for my painkillers. I slowly opened my eyes when I felt the weight of his body depress the side of my bed.

"Here you go. Open your hand," he slipped the pills in it and handed me a glass of water. "I also brought an ice pack for your head. Where should I lay it?"

"Here. On my right side," I placed my hand on the welcomed cold pack and squeezed my eyes shut. I willed myself to stop crying.

"Try and get some sleep. You'll be better in the morning. I'm here if you need anything," he rubbed his finger down my arm softly and then walked back around to his side of the bed.

THE BRIGHT SUNLIGHT hurt my eyes as I opened them a slight crack.

"I'm sorry I woke you. Go back to sleep. I got the Littles breakfast and am taking Chase to his basketball game. I'll be home shortly. Try and get some sleep. The other two are fine," Josh bent and kissed my head before leaving, softly closing the door behind him.

My stomach lurched and I threw back the covers and raced to

the toilet. I retched but nothing came up. My head felt like it was splitting in half and no position could give me comfort. I lay on the cool tile of my bathroom floor for about 30 minutes before I mustered the energy to go out to the family room.

"Hi, Momma. How are you feeling?" Carter asked as soon as he saw me.

"Hi, baby. How are you doing? Where's your sister?"

"Good. She's in her room playing. I was just getting a snack."

"OK, I need to lie down for a minute. My head hurts," I slowly limped to the couch and laid down on the chaise lounge part. I started gasping for air and I heard noises come out of me that sounded animal-like.

Carter came over to where I was laying and his eyes got big.

"Should I go get Kris? What do I do, Momma?"

"I'm sorry I'm scaring you, Carter. I'm in so much pain! Can you call Dad and tell him to come right home?" I handed him my cell phone and continued to weep.

I closed my eyes but could hear him make the call.

"Dad. You have to come home right away. Something is wrong with Mom," he paused. "OK. Bye."

"He said that he'll be here in three minutes," Carter placed his cool hand on my arm.

"Thanks, baby. I'll be all right," I whispered trying to soothe him.

The door slammed and Josh came rushing in. I was hyperventilating and my upper lip was covered in beads of sweat.

"Kater, I'm here." He sat down behind me and pulled me into his arms, "Shh. Just relax and focus on normal breathing. Try and stop crying. That's it. You're doing it."

I rocked in his arms and tried to concentrate on my breathing. My hand was pushing firmly on my head, willing it not to explode.

We stayed in that position for over an hour; Josh holding me, quieting me, comforting me.

I could feel my children standing in front of me and heard Josh quietly tell them, "Momma's gonna be alright," before I finally drifted off to sleep.

TWELVE

December 2013

THE NEXT DAY after my steroid fiasco, my head had finally stopped trying to come off my body. I stopped the steroids after talking with my brother about the side effects.

I climbed into the shower and turned the water to hot. I felt "off" and hoped that the steam would help to lift the fog. Pulling down the shampoo bottle, I flipped open the lid and tried to squeeze some into my hand. All I felt in my left hand was needles. It was numb. I shook it out and tested my right hand. It was the same. Both hands were numb and I realized I couldn't feel up to my elbows.

I quickly shut the water off and got out without washing up. Plucking my phone off the counter, I thumbed a text to Randy.

Me: *Hey sorry to bother you on a Sunday. Both of my arms are numb now. Is it from my neck?*

Randy: *Both arms? Can you feel your hands?*

Me: *No*

Randy: *You need to go to the ER*

Me: *Ok. I will now. Thank you!*

Randy: *Pls keep me posted.*

Grabbing some workout clothes, I threw them on and whipped my hair up into a ponytail. I slipped my phone into my pocket and went to find Josh.

"J!" I called.

"Hey, babe. I thought you were getting a shower?"

"I was, but you need to take me to the ER."

"Hmm. OK. Why?"

"My hands and arms are numb. Both of them. Randy said I need to get checked out. Can you take me please?"

"Sure, let me grab my wallet. Hey kids, I'll be right back. I'm going to run your mom to the ER."

Chase padded over to me in his bare feet. "What's up, Mom? Why are you going to the ER?"

"It's my back. I think. I'll be fine. Can you please watch your brother and sister until Dad gets back?"

"Sure. I love you."

"I love you more," I said. I smiled at him and lifted my purse onto my shoulder.

JOSH PULLED THE car up to the entrance of the emergency room. I opened my door and set my foot on the ground.

"Just call me when you're done and I'll pick you up. I love you. Let me know what they say."

"I will. I love you," I leaned over and gave him a quick peck on his lips. I didn't want the kids to be around all of the sick people in the ER. I hoped I wouldn't be here all day.

The place was packed as I walked through the double glass doors. I waited in the small line that had formed at the check-in desk.

"Name please?" the nurse at the desk asked.

"Catherine Mathias," I said getting my insurance card out and ready.

"What issues are you having today?"

Where do I start?

"Pain and numbness extending down both of my legs and just started in my arms and hands. Bad headache," I explained.

She rattled off a list of questions and symptoms.

"Oh, and I recently had a stroke. I'm slightly worried maybe I'm having another one with his head pain and pain in my arm."

"I'm going to have you come back for an EKG. It'll be just a few moments dear. Just wait off to the side there," she pointed to the area next to the door. "There are people in front of you but if you're having a heart attack we need to check right now. Just a moment please..."

Moving off to the side, I sighed. Almost immediately, a woman pushed through the door and called my name.

"Hi, you need to come with me. I'm going to do an EKG on you to check on your heart."

I nodded and followed her to a small room. She quickly put the blood pressure cuff on me and pumped it up. I watched as the little gauge spun around.

"151 over 92. You're tachycardia."

"I'm usually very low like 106 over 68. I'm in pain so that's probably making it go so high," I explained.

"Let's get you hooked up to see about your heart," she moved around me swiftly, placing pads on my chest.

The EKG came back normal, which was a relief.

"OK, honey, can you please give me some health history?"

I ran down through the list of my health.

"Is that all?"

"Oh, and I was told I have a mass on my right frontal lobe a year ago but they said it was caused from a stroke."

She put down her pen, "You're just now adding that in?" She shook her head. "You're not very good at this health history, are you?"

I smiled weakly at her, "I guess not."

"It's okay, dear. I'm going to get you a room as quickly as I can. There are about forty people in front of you, though, so it may take some time."

"I understand. Thank you for your help," I stood.

"Follow me back out to the waiting room. Someone will be calling you shortly to draw some labs."

Walking back out to the room with the swarm of people, I moved to the area that was the quietest. My head was pounding and I hoped that I wouldn't be here all day. I texted Josh and gave him an update. He and the kids were fine.

As the day passed on, I watched the people slowly start to clear out of the room. I was finally called to meet with the doctor. She wanted to do an MRI of my lower back to see if I had a herniated or ruptured disk causing the numbness.

The doctor ordered a lower back scan. I shifted my weight in the uncomfortable orange chair while I waited for my MRI to be read. I tried to close my eyes and sleep sitting up but my back and head had other plans.

"Catherine Mathias?"

My name was finally called and I followed the nurse back to a room, taking a seat in a reclining chair.

"Hi, Catherine. I'm Dr. A."

"Hi, I'm Kate. So do I have a herniated disk?" I asked.

The doctor glanced down at the papers she was holding. "Actually, no. Your scan is clear."

I looked into her face and noticed the puzzled look.

"If it's clear, then what's causing all of this pain?"

"I'm not sure yet. I want to do a mid-back as well as a neck and brain MRI to rule out any other problems higher up. You did this exercising?"

"Yeah, I was doing Orange Theory. Have you heard of it?"

"Yes, I used to do it, too, before I hurt my back and had to have surgery. I'm familiar with your pain," she smiled down at me.

"Then you know the intensity?"

"Of course," she made a note on her clipboard, "I'm going to order that mid-back MRI now and we'll see what's going on."

"OK, can I get something to eat while I'm waiting? I'm starving."

"I know you've had a long wait today. I apologize for that. Let's not eat just yet. I want to make sure that you don't have to go into surgery if something comes back on this next MRI. I'll get it scheduled right away and we should have answers about an hour after."

"Thank you."

"Hang tight. Someone will come and get you shortly."

I nodded and crossed my legs while I waited.

⌐⌐⌐⌐⌐⌐⌐⌐⌐⌐⌐⌐⌐⌐⌐

MY PHONE BUZZED in my hand and I glanced up at the clock on the wall. It was just after 9:00 p.m.

A text came in from Josh.

Josh: *Any update?*

Me: *Just had my second MRI. Still waiting...*

Josh: *K. Keep me posted. Kids in bed.*

Me: *Luv u!*

Josh: *Luv u!*

The curtain that separated the small room from the others parted and Dr. A walked through.

"Hey, Dr. A. Did you get my results back?"

"They just came across," she was clenching my papers in her hand and came closer to where I was sitting. "The MRI is clear."

"What? How can that be?"

"Well, it means that there are no herniated disks but something else is causing your numbness and pain," she fidgeted with some lint on her white jacket.

"Something else like what?" I asked.

"I want to do a neck and brain MRI to check for MS," she stopped talking and looked at me.

A good friend of my mom's had just died from complications of MS. Multiple sclerosis is a horrible disease.

"We do a scan of the brain to check for any lesions that would be caused by the disease. Many of your symptoms fit... changes in urination, pain and numbness in your limbs, weakness, fatigue."

My eyes welled up with tears. I swallowed and looked up at her.

"I can't have MS. I have three kids and my husband is always gone. I have to be able to function on my own. I just can't have it," I wrung my hands in my lap.

Her eyes were also wet and I realized that she was getting upset about my case. That both broke my heart and filled it at the same time.

"I know. Believe me, I know. I'm going to admit you tonight so we can get these tests done. If you go home, it may take weeks to get the MRIs and then the results. Does that work?"

I quickly ran Josh's schedule through my mind. This happened to be his home week.

"Yes. That will work."

"OK, a room just opened up on the fourth floor. I'll have someone come get you and move you up there. In the meantime, I'll be praying for you Kate," she bent down and embraced me.

Having her warm arms wrapped around me, if only briefly, calmed me. She gave one last tighter squeeze and released me.

"Thank you. I appreciate the prayers." I smiled weakly at her.

"I hope the doctors can get something figured out for you. Selina will be coming to get you to take you to your room. Take good care."

Picking up my phone, I quickly punched in Josh's number. He answered on the first ring.

"Are you moving in?"

"Ha. Kinda. They want to admit me so they can do some more tests." I filled him in on what was to be done and the possibility of MS. "Hey, can you please bring me some clean clothes, my glasses, and toothbrush?"

"Why? It's not like you didn't shower today," he laughed on the other end.

"I didn't! I feel nasty. I'll text you my room number as soon as I get up there. How long til you'll be here?"

"About 20 minutes. See you soon."

I hung up the phone just as a sweet older lady wheeled a wheelchair into where I was sitting.

"Hi, Catherine. I'm Selina. I'll be your ride to your room," she smiled and put on the brakes on the chair.

"Hello, Selina. Thank you," I climbed in the chair and lifted my feet up so she could put down the foot rests.

The ride up to the fourth floor was quick and cold.

"Why is it so freezing in here?" I asked.

"They keep it cold so bacteria can't live as well. Also, all of the machinery puts off a lot of heat. You get used to it after a while."

I climbed out of the wheelchair and was greeted by Brian.

"Hi, Catherine. I'm the night nurse and will be helping you until 7:00 a.m. Here's a gown for you to put on and some booties."

"Thanks, Brian. Can I grab a quick shower first?" No sooner had I said that when I saw Josh walk up behind Brian.

"I wouldn't let her. She's trouble," Josh teased to Brian.

Brian turned around and cocked his head to one side.

"He's teasing. This is my husband," I reached my hand out to Josh. "Hi, babe."

"Oh, well in that case, yes, you can shower. I'm not sure when they'll come get you for the MRIs."

"They're going to do those tonight?" I questioned looking at the clock and seeing that it was already 10:30 p.m.

"Yes, they do it whenever the machines are free. It'll be good to get it done tonight because we share the MRI machine with the ER and you never know how many traumas will come in and have to use it. I'll be back to get you when they're ready," Brian closed the door behind him.

Josh handed me a small bag. I unzipped it and started pulling out my toothbrush and some clean clothes.

"Thank you. I feel disgusting. How was your night?"

"Day was good. I had no idea you would be here so long. How are you holding up?"

"I'm OK. Just super tired and my head and back hurt."

"I'm sorry, babe. Why don't you get a shower and try and get some sleep?"

"I will. Kiss the kids for me. I'll call you when I'm released."

"When will that be?" Josh asked.

"I'm hoping tomorrow?"

"Sounds good. I love you, Kater."

"I love you," I hugged him and gave him a kiss before he left.

CLIMBING INTO BED, I hit the overhead light and the room became pitch black. My shower had felt so good to get off the grime and germs from sitting in the ER all day.

The door creaked open and Brian popped his head in.

"Hi, sorry to wake you, but they're ready for you to get your MRI."

I sat up in bed and pushed the button so the light above the bed clicked on.

"Now? It's midnight."

"Yep. Is that OK?"

"If they're ready then I am, too," I pulled back the warm covers and the cool air hit my legs. "Brrr. I'm freezing!"

I started to get up and Brian stopped me.

"Actually, I'll be taking you down in your bed."

"Seriously? That's kinda cool." I watched as he undid some of the monitors and unplugged the bed. He slowly pushed me out of the room and down the hallway.

"It helps people from falling and getting hurt. And is more comfortable for the patients, too."

"Makes sense."

"Here we are. Radiation and Imaging. They'll call me when you're finished."

"Thanks, Brian," I smiled at the man with the light brown hair.

"Hi, Catherine. I'm Derek and will be taking you back in just a minute. Can I get you a warmed blanket?"

"Now we're talking! Yes, please."

Derek draped the warm blanket over my body and I instantly shivered.

"I wish I could do this at home. It's a little bit of heaven right here," I sighed.

"You can—do it at home. Just take a blanket and put it in the microwave for say about 20 seconds. It'll warm right up!"

I lifted one eyebrow and glanced at him to see if he was joking. Surely that was a fire just waiting to happen. His face was still and not smiling.

"OK. I'll have to try that," I replied. "Not ever," I muttered under my breath.

"They're ready for you. Let's get you up on the table. Have you had an MRI before?"

"Yes, just a few hours ago," I grinned at him. "And no, I'm not claustrophobic."

"Good, our technician will be doing a neck and brain MRI.

Should take about an hour and a half." He slipped earphones on me and snapped the white cover that fits over your head to lock you in place.

"What type of music do you want to listen to?"

"How about Christmas music? It is only 16 days away as my daughter told me today," I closed my eyes and tried to relax as I moved slowly into the tube.

THIRTEEN

Dr. Kah Yu

THE SUNLIGHT STREAMED through the window and was only slightly filtered by the flimsy window shade. I reached over and grabbed my glasses that were perched on the side table. I slipped them on and glanced at the clock: 7:02 a.m.

By the time I had finished the MRIs, it was after 2:00 a.m., so I hadn't gotten much sleep. Sighing, I could hear the hospital already coming to life outside my door.

As I pushed the covers back off my legs, I heard my cell phone beep with a notification from Facebook. My feet hit the cold tile floor and I shivered. Moving over to the small desk on the opposite side of the room, I unzipped the bag to see what clothes Josh had packed for me.

"Typical," I said out loud and laughed. Nothing matched except for one light lavender workout shirt and some black yoga pants. I grabbed my phone and sent a text to Josh.

Me: *Morning! None of my clothes match.*

Josh: *Who's going to see you anyway? ;)*

Me: *True. How are the kids?*

Josh: *Good, getting them bfast now. Call you later. Luv u!*

Me: *Luv u!*

Since I had showered so late last night, I threw on the clothes and trudged into the bathroom. My stomach growled as I brushed my teeth. I hadn't eaten much the day before and didn't have a lot of fat reserves.

Quickly swiping on some mascara so I didn't look dead, I dusted my nose with some powder and added some lip gloss. Popping my contacts into my eyes so I could see better, I put my glasses back in their case. My hair was long and hit just past my bra strap. I pulled my brush through it and then twisted it to the side into a braid.

I flipped off the light and was sitting back on the bed when the curtain in front of my door moved aside and in walked my neighbor and friend Kris. He was wearing his light green scrubs and had a badge hanging around his neck.

"Hey, good morning! What're you doing here?" I asked, smiling up at him.

"Shayla talked to Josh and found out you were here. How are you?"

"I'm hanging in there. They did a bunch of tests and MRIs. I'm still waiting on results."

"Keep me posted on what they find out. Text me if you need anything."

"Thank you. I will do. I hope to go home today, but until then

I'm pretending like this is a staycation."

Kris laughed, "Whatever works! I'm off to the office. I'll check back in with you soon."

"Thank you for coming by. Were you here anyway?"

"Yeah, I already did my rounds and now have to go to the office before some surgeries later today."

"It's early! What time did you start?" I asked him.

"Four-thirty. Just a typical day for me," he grinned.

"That's brutal. Have a good day—and Kris, thank you."

"Not a problem. See ya!" He moved the curtain aside and I heard the wooden door click behind him.

The remote for the TV was attached to the bed and I picked it up and flipped on the television. The door creaked open again and I looked over to see a woman carrying a tray with breakfast.

"Good morning! I have your breakfast," she set the tray on the small table that extended over the bed.

"Hi. Thank goodness. I'm starving," I pulled the lid off the hot plate and my stomach grumbled when the smell of pancakes and sausage wafted up to my nose.

"Can I get you anything else?"

"No, this is great. Thank you," I immediately poured the syrup over the steaming stack of pancakes and forked some into my mouth.

I must've been starving because the food tasted so good. Either that or because I didn't have to cook it, the food tasted even better.

I checked my Facebook as I was eating and could hear the quiet chatter of the TV on in the background. I never watched anything in the mornings as I was getting the kids ready for school so I didn't even know what channel to put it on.

The day slowly ticked by... lunch was served and nurses were in and out of my room checking my vitals. As much as I sometimes craved alone time, I was starting to get tired of sitting around by myself. I wasn't used to having so much down time.

I picked up the phone and called Josh.

"Hey, babe. How're you doing?"

"I'm bored. What are you doing?" I asked.

"Working."

"Oh. Can you come down here and work on your blackberry?"

"I have a lot of calls to make. I'll probably be down later to pick you up anyway. Have you talked to a doctor yet?"

"No. Not yet. OK, I just thought that—" I was interrupted when my door opened and an Asian man with glasses walked into my room.

"Babe, I gotta go. A doctor just walked in," I explained.

"OK, call me later," Josh hung up the phone.

"Hi, sorry about that," I apologized to the doctor and smiled.

"Hello, Catherine, I'm Dr. Yu. I'm the neurologist assigned to your case," he said moving over to the computer monitor that was on the right-hand side of my bed.

"Alright. It's nice to meet you. I'm Kate." I figured no sense in beating around the bush and got right to the point. "Do I have MS?"

"That can't be determined quite yet. We did find something on your brain MRI, however. You have a mass on your right frontal lobe," he explained, pushing his glasses up on his face.

"Oh, that. I know. I had a stroke a year ago."

"This doesn't look like a stroke. It looks like a tumor."

I waved my hand, dismissing his statement. My other neurologist told me I had a stroke. Surely, he wouldn't have missed a brain tumor.

"It can be one of three things. One," he held his pointer finger in the air, "a brain tumor. Two, MS. Three, a stroke, but it doesn't look like a stroke. It looks like a cluster of cotton balls."

I squinted my eyes and tried to take in what he was telling me, still not quite believing this new theory. I had MS not a brain tumor.

"So if it's a brain tumor, what do we do? How do we find out for sure?"

"I need to run some more tests and do a spinal tap. The fluid in the spine can give us more information if it is indeed MS, but I really think it's a tumor."

Uh-huh. A brain tumor. Right.

It wasn't that I was questioning what this new doctor was telling me... OK, yes I was, but I was struggling with the information because I never questioned the other neurologist. In hindsight, I should've. I should've gotten a second opinion when having a stroke didn't really fit my symptoms and me.

Now, as I look back, I realize how important it is to trust your gut and when things don't feel right, they probably aren't. But having a brain tumor? That seemed so severe. So scary. So deadly. I didn't want to believe what Dr. Yu was suggesting.

I nodded my head and looked at this man standing in front of me with dark, kind eyes. Little did I know at the time that he would be the one that saved me; he would be the one that got it right.

I don't believe in accidents. Everything happens for a reason, even the dark days. Sometimes bad has to happen to realize that there is goodness and light that comes out of everything. My dark days were just beginning, but Dr. Yu standing in front of me telling me that I had a 33 percent chance of having a brain tumor was not an accident. It was a God thing.

I was the last patient that Dr. Yu would see who had been admitted from the ER. His wife had told him that she didn't want him to take calls anymore after the end of the year. It was December 10 and I was the last one he would ever be called to round on from the ER. That wasn't an accident. Dr. Yu was sent to save my life.

We chatted for a while about my health. I gave him the background on my history and he listened intently.

My phone starting buzzing lying next to me.

"You can get that," Dr. Yu told me.

I flipped it over and saw it was Josh calling.

"No, it's just my husband. He can wait," I smiled up at this man I was starting to feel so comfortable around.

"I'm going to order a spinal tap for you and run a few more tests. I'll be back to check on you tomorrow."

"OK, and thank you Dr. Yu," I smiled at him, "Have a good afternoon."

"You, too," he turned and pushed back the curtain.

I called Josh and left a voicemail telling him that it looked like I would be staying for a while longer. I didn't tell him about the possible brain tumor. That would wait until I could tell him in person.

I swung my legs over the bed and walked the few feet to the window. Pressing my hand on the cool glass, I looked down into the fountain a few stories below me. People were sitting on the benches and the sun was shining brightly. The world was moving on while I was trying to deal with the fact that my world might be drastically changing.

FOURTEEN

Doctors, doctors, and more doctors

LEANING AGAINST THE wall, my left hand went to my lower back and I squeezed it, slowly massaging the tight muscles. I turned when I heard the door open.

A man walked through the doorway wearing a vest over his blue scrubs.

Thinking he was a nurse or technician I said to him, "Hi, are you here to take me for more tests?"

"No, I'm Dr. N. I'm the urologist who has been assigned to your case. Do you mind coming and lying down? I need to ask you some questions."

I walked over to the small bed and plopped down.

He compressed his hands on my stomach. "Does this hurt?"

"No."

"How about this?" his hands moved across my abdomen and he asked me about my symptoms.

"We need to have a look inside at your bladder to see what is causing the thickening wall. We'll schedule an appointment when you're released. Do you know yet when you're going home?"

Ah, yes. Bladder cancer. I had forgotten about that little treat with the new brain tumor possibility.

"I'm not sure yet. A few of the doctors are saying MS. What're your thoughts?"

He nodded, "I would agree with that based on your symptoms."

"My neurologist has ordered a spinal tap to find out more."

"Good plan. I'm going to leave my card. Please call and schedule your appointment when you're released."

I took the card from his outstretched hand and put it on the bedside table, "I will. Thank you, doctor."

The nurse came in and had a tray filled with vials. The doctor left silently and the nurse scanned my wrist ID.

"I need to draw some more blood. Sorry, Kate," she started wiping alcohol on the crook of my elbow.

"It's OK. More tests?"

She nodded, "You'll feel a slight poke."

"That's what they all say," I chuckled and she smiled.

"That'll do it. I'll get these to the lab," she pushed her cart out of the room leaving me alone.

My cell phone buzzed and I glanced down at the incoming text from Tanya.

Tanya: *How's it going, sis?*

Me: *Doctors are saying MS. New neurologist is saying brain tumor. :(*

Tanya: *OMG! Are you serious?*

Me: *Yeah, it's crazy. Either way, I guess I'm messed up. Haha*

Tanya: *Way to stay positive. I can tell you're in a good frame of mind.*

Me: *I'm trying. Come and bust me outta here!*

Tanya: *I'm on a business trip but I think Alexa and Denise are coming to visit you soon and bring you a little happy gift. Love you, girl.*

Me: *Love you more. Will keep you posted.*

My door pushed open and my new nurse came rushing in. She started checking my charts and scanned my ID. Her fingers quickly typed over the keyboard.

"What's going on? Did you find out something?"

"Some blood work came back and you may have West Nile..." she left that bomb and promptly walked out of my room.

"What? Hey come back! West Nile? I have West Nile virus?"

No answer.

Screw this.

I grabbed my phone and quickly typed in West Nile virus and did a search. While I was waiting for it to pull up my mind started racing. Josh and I had gone to Jamaica the month prior with my sister and her husband. Had I gotten West Nile there?

WebMD pulled up the symptoms and my eyes scanned the document.

Fever, headache, body aches, stiff neck, sleepiness.

Possible death.

What the hell?

I quickly punched in my brother's number and called him.

"Hey, Kater. What's up?"

"Bill, a nurse just came in and said I may have West Nile. I can't have that. I could die. How would I have West Nile..." my words came rushing out.

"Calm down. Who said that, a doctor?"

"No, a nurse rushed in and said it and then left before I could ask her anything."

"So you haven't talked to a doctor yet?" he asked.

"Not yet but I did—" I was interrupted when my door opened and a stout man came in.

"Bill, a doctor just came in. I'll talk to you later."

I disconnected the phone and my eyes looked upon the new face. He had thinning hair and a large mole on his left cheek.

"Hello, I'm Dr. L, an infectious disease doctor."

"Oh, good Lord. Then it's true what they're saying? Do I have West Nile virus?"

"Listen. Don't listen to what those douchebags are saying. A hundred different doctors could come up with a hundred different educated guesses. Don't latch on to one doctor's idea of what you have."

I laughed out loud, surprised that he had called doctors douchebags. But I immediately felt a sense of relief wash over me.

"Whew! So I don't have West Nile? Do I have MS?"

"I'm not sure what you have. Your white blood count and nucleolus numbers are elevated. We can't find the source of infection, but these numbers show that you have one."

"I don't have a fever though," I responded.

"I see that." He glanced down at the papers in his hand.

"Do you think I have MS? That's been the consensus lately."

"It's a high probability. You have a spinal tap scheduled for tomorrow at 11 a.m. I see. That'll give us a better idea of what we're dealing with."

"My spinal tap is tomorrow? So much for going home today..."

"You can't eat for a few hours before you have it and I see you just had dinner. I've run every test I can think of and nothing else is showing up. I think you need to relax and not get so worked up. We need to wait for the results of the spinal and go from there."

I liked this guy. He was real and telling me straight.

"OK, I can do that. Thanks, Dr. L."

"Never a problem. I'll be back by tomorrow after we get back some more results. Have a good night."

I squeezed my eyes shut tightly and inhaled deeply. I held my breath for a moment and then blew it out.

Sending a text to my brother, I told him the latest news. I also sent a text to Kris and asked him about Dr. L. He told me that Dr. L is like that and says stuff like that all the time and has been known to call people douchebags to their face.

Next, I called Josh and told him about what Dr. Yu had said about the brain tumor, about West Nile, and that I wasn't coming home today. After hanging up with Josh, I laid back on my pillows and flipped through the channels as I settled in for the night.

I WAS STARTING to go crazy in the hospital room and had slept fitfully during the night. Nurses would come in to get my vitals and wake me periodically. I woke early and jumped in the shower before my spinal tap.

When I left the bathroom, there was my breakfast tray sitting next to my bed. My stomach growled when the smell of scrambled eggs hit my nostrils.

I couldn't eat before the test and also couldn't stand to have the food in front of me. Yes, it was hospital food, but my stomach didn't realize that. I clutched the tray with both hands and walked to the door, determined to get rid of it before my stomach ate itself.

The door swung open and my nurse walked in.

"Oh, are you finished? I can take that for you," she took the tray from my hands.

"No, but I have a spinal in a bit and can't eat," I explained.

"Oh, dear. I'm sorry. The breakfast staff didn't know that. Let me get it out of here for you. Someone will be by shortly to take you down."

I nodded and watched as she left the room. I looked up at the analog clock on the wall and noted the time. Josh should have the kids to school by now.

I dialed his number and he answered out of breath.

"Hey, what are you doing?" he panted.

"What are you doing?"

"Just finishing a run with your pony."

"Ahh. Is he tired yet?" I asked knowing that Josh would take Buddy on 5-mile runs and Buddy acted like it was a few steps. He had endless energy.

"Nope, not even close. How's today looking to come home?"

"I'm not sure yet. They're coming soon to get me soon for the spinal tap. If I don't get home today, you need to come down and bring the kids. Please," I pleaded with him. I needed to see him and my babies.

"I will, hon. I was planning on it," I could hear him smiling.

"OK, thank you. I'll see you this afternoon then."

"I thought we would come down after dinner. Does that work?"

"That's fine. I'm actually getting tired of watching movies," I laughed. "Careful what you wish for."

"Hang in there. I love you," Josh replied.

"I love you," I punched the red disconnect button and put my phone on the desk. It was getting close to 1 p.m. and I figured they would be coming to get me soon for the spinal tap. So much for my eleven o'clock appointment time. I wasn't too excited about the test and worried how much it would hurt.

Almost as soon as I finished the thought, a male nurse came in to take me down.

"Hi, I'm Rick to take you to get a CT before your spinal."

"Hi, Rick. Do you need me to get back in my bed?"

"Yes, I'll transport you that way."

I walked slowly over to the bed as my back and head hurt more today. It didn't help that I hadn't been doing much of anything the last few days except lying in that tiny hospital bed watching TV. I was stiff and sore from not using my muscles. I climbed into bed and covered my legs up to my waist with the thin blanket.

The wheels creaked as they begin moving down the shiny tile hallway. I watched as the bright fluorescent lights overhead passed me one by one.

Rick carefully maneuvered my bed through the double wooden doors and we came to a stop. I leaned up and propped myself on my elbows.

"The CT won't take long and then I'll take you from here down to the spinal tap," Rick helped me up and I walked over to the CT machine.

"Hey, Robbie, this is Catherine for her CT."

Robbie looked up from his paperwork, "Great. Catherine, go ahead and lay on the table. Have you had a CT before?"

"Not today," I grinned at him. "Yes, I just had one a few days ago along with some MRIs. And no, I'm not claustrophobic."

"OK, good enough. This will just take a few minutes."

The scan was quick and painless and when it was over, Rick

helped me back to my bed. He wheeled me down to where they would be doing the spinal tap. We rolled into the room and it was darker than the brightly lit hallway.

Two young women were finishing something in the small room at the back and I could see their mouths moving through the little glass window. The brunette looked up and saw us and waved.

The blonde woman with her hair pulled into a sleek ponytail addressed us first, "Thanks, Rick. We should be done in about an hour. I'll call you when she's ready to be taken back up to her room."

"That works. See you soon," Rick left me and pushed back through the doors.

"Hello, Catherine. Will this be your first spinal tap?"

"Yes. And you can call me Kate. I'm nervous. Does it hurt?" I asked the brunette.

Both women were already busy moving around the room getting it ready. To my left was a table with a large X-ray machine above it. Again, it was freezing in here.

"I've never had one, but some people complain it's the worst pain they've ever felt and others say it's not too bad," the brunette nurse replied pulling out a green hospital gown.

"That's reassuring... like not at all," I replied with a smile.

The blonde nurse walked over to where I was now sitting up.

"I'm Stacy and you're going to be just fine. Dr. M is very skilled at doing this. It may be uncomfortable but won't last long."

"What's your definition of long?"

"Usually about 15-20 minutes, depending on how well the fluid drains," Stacy explained.

"Drains? What exactly will he be doing?"

The brunette handed me the hospital gown, "Kate, why don't you get changed into this lovely gown and then we'll explain more. I think the doctor is on his way."

Stacy said, "Go ahead and take everything off from the waist up. We'll just be getting the instruments ready in the back room and will be right back."

I stripped off my shirt and bra, folded them into a pile, and put them at the foot of my bed. I took off my pants and pulled on some socks with grippers on the bottom. At least my feet would be warm.

I climbed back in bed and quickly covered up but not before a shiver went through my body.

The ladies were laughing about something and I smiled hearing their laughter. I took a deep breath and tried to relax.

"Are you all set, Kate?" Stacy asked me as they came back into the room.

"Yep, I guess so."

"So what's going to happen is the doctor will give you some topical anesthetic on your skin. Once that's taken effect, he'll stick a needle into your spinal column to collect some fluid. It'll feel like a pinch unless he hits a nerve," she explained while she draped the table with a cloth.

"What happens if he hits a nerve?" I asked.

"It's like an electric shock that will go down your legs."

"That sounds pleasurable," I responded. "Have I told you how excited I am about this?" I smiled lopsided.

They both laughed. The brunette said reassuringly, "It's over quickly and he is the best at what he does."

"Speaking of—here he is," Stacey moved the tray of instruments closer to the table.

"Good morning, Catherine. I'm Dr. M and I'll be doing your spinal tap. I just finished reading your reports and I see that you have a mass in your brain."

"Hello. Yes, I had a stroke about a year ago. Or I have MS. That's what the consensus seems to be."

"I'm not confident that it's either of those. Have the ladies explained the process that we're going to be doing today?"

"Yes, I do want to tell you that I have scoliosis, so my spine curves about 10 degrees to the right. I'm not sure if that makes a difference or not."

"I'll look at it in a moment. Go ahead and come over to this table. I'll be using a live X-ray to view into your spinal column while I'm working. After we complete the test, you'll need to lay flat on your back for 30 minutes." Dr. M explained. He pulled on his latex gloves as I walked over to the table.

"I'll be making a small hole and some of the spinal fluid can leak out causing a pretty intense spinal headache. Staying on your back will help your own blood to clot and fill that hole."

"What if it doesn't? I mean close the hole? Then what?" I asked.

"Then we have to go in and help it with a small surgery."

"Lovely," I replied weakly.

"It helps with the headache if you drink Coke," Stacy told me.

"Why?" I asked.

"That's what patients say to drink a lot of fluid to help replenish what we take and the Coca-Cola helps with the headache."

"OK, I can do that."

"I need you to lie facedown on the table. You can turn your head to the right slightly. You need to stay very still," Dr. M instructed.

Doing as I was told, I climbed onto the table and turned my head so I was looking at the wall.

"I'm going to rub a little anesthetic on your back," Dr. M explained as I felt the cold liquid drop onto my skin. "I'll incline the table at about a 45-degree angle. Can you feel that? It should just feel like pressure."

"I feel something but I'm OK. Go ahead," I saw the needle out of the corner of my eye and it looked like one that's in horror movies. I swear it was about 8-inches long and I squeezed my eyes shut in anticipation.

"I need you to relax now. Here we go..." Dr. M peered into the goggles on the machine above me and I felt the needle pierce my skin.

Damn, that hurts!

"OK, Catherine, I'm in. Next I'm going to—"

"Oh, oww!" I tried not to scream it but the words flew out of my mouth loudly. I felt like I had been electrified and it shot down my left leg and out my foot.

"Did you just have a volt?"

"Yes, and it still hurts."

"I'm going to pull the needle out just a little then. Hold on," he slowly pulled back the needle, "There. Is that better?"

"Yes," I half whispered.

"I need to incline the table so we can get the fluid collected. You're doing well. Not too much longer," he explained as I felt my top half being lifted up.

No words were being spoken and I tried to concentrate on something else. I thought about my kids, Josh, the sunshine warming my face.

"Catherine? I'm not getting enough fluid. I'm going to have to incline you some more. Ready?"

The table slowly moved upward again and I had the feeling that I would slide right down and off of it. My right hand was near the edge and I gripped on to the table, holding on for dear life.

"Kate, you won't fall. It just feels that way. You're safe," Stacy assured me.

Dr. M continued to look in his goggles in the machine.

"You prefer to go by Kate?" he asked.

I slightly nodded my head, afraid to move much and cause more pressure in my back than I was already feeling.

"Well, Kate, the good news is moving you up has helped and the fluid is collecting more readily now. Shouldn't be too much longer now."

I started to count the seconds thinking that would help time pass more quickly and I would forget about the giant needle piercing my back right now. It didn't help. Just about the time when I was going to ask how much longer, Dr. M pulled back from the machine.

"We got it. We got enough. We're all done. I'm going to slowly withdraw the needle and you'll be finished," he did as he said and then covered the hole with a bandage. He pulled the gown back down to cover me and the nurses were quick to move.

My hospital bed was rolled up next to the table and I realized I was still gripping the edge for life.

The brunette instructed, "We are going to help you move back to your bed. We need to go slowly and have you flat on your back," she lowered the table so it was level with my bed.

I rolled from my stomach slowly to my back. Their hands guided me as I scooted across the hard table and straight over to the bed.

Stacy quickly covered me and tucked the blanket around my feet.

"This is the position you need to stay in for at least 30 minutes."

"OK, I will. What time is it now?" I asked.

"It's four o'clock."

"Four o'clock?" I questioned. I knew that had come to get me later than 11 a.m., but how had that much time passed? "I'll stay flat—and doctor? How long before you have the results?"

"It takes 72 hours to get the results," he explained. "Take care."

Rick poked his head in the door. "Is she ready to go back up?"

"She's ready," Stacy wheeled me over to the door and laid her hand on my right foot. "I hope they find some answers for you."

"Thank you. So do I." I smiled and felt my bed already starting to make its creaky way back down the hall.

"So was it as bad as people say?" Rick asked me on the way back.

"It wasn't pleasant, but it wasn't the worst pain I've ever felt. Hey, I missed breakfast and lunch today and I'm starving. Could you see about getting my dinner delivered soon?"

"Sure, I saw on the schedule that they were bringing it at five o'clock."

"That's perfect. I can't sit up for another 30 minutes anyway. Can you please bring me some water and Coke? The nurses said that would help with the possible headache."

"Absolutely. Just let me get your bed plugged back in and I'll be right back," he hurriedly put the brakes on my bed and plugged the cords back in. "Here's your remote," Rick put it in my hand.

"Thanks," I pushed the button and the TV roared to life. I couldn't see the screen but I could hear the sound. "What is this?"

"It says it's *The Perfect Game.* I'll go get your water and Coke."

The minutes passed slowly as I listened to the movie and sipped on my water and Coke through a straw. Multiple times, I dribbled on my chin and gown trying to drink without moving my back.

I need to go to the bathroom.

I could see the clock on the wall and saw that it was 4:20 p.m. Still having 10 minutes before I could get up, I told myself I could wait to go.

No, I can't. I have to go now.

I depressed my call button.

"This is Anna. How can I help you?" a sweet voice boomed over my speaker.

"Hey, Anna, I have to go to the bathroom. Badly. I'm not supposed to get up for 10 more minutes because I just had a spinal tap. Am I close enough?"

"Actually, no. You can't get up for 10 more minutes. Is it an emergency?" she asked.

"Yes. Yes, it is!"

"Alright, I'll be right down with a bed pan."

"Uh, OK. Thank you," I croaked.

Freaking fantastic. This day can't get any better.

My door opened swiftly and a pretty woman with sandy brown hair in a ponytail whisked in.

"Hi. Oh, thank God. I'm about to have a mess to clean up," I semi-shouted. And then my mouth wouldn't stop running. "I had the spinal tap and they said to drink a lot of fluid to help it replenish. So I did," I waved my hand at the empty glasses on the tray. "Please help me. I'm about to explode."

She grinned at me, "Have you ever used a bed pan before?"

"I can't say I've had the pleasure."

Anna chuckled. She helped to get it situated under me.

"Go ahead and go. I'll move behind the curtain and give you some privacy. Just tell me when you're done."

"OK... this is weird," I kinda groaned but instantly felt relief. After what seemed like five minutes and I was still going, I started to laugh.

"Why am I still going? I can't stop!" I asked Anna.

"It's normal. You don't have gravity to help you go. This is normal," she explained waiting patiently behind the curtain.

"Oh, good Lord. I think I'm done. Now what?"

She came around the side of the bed, "Do you need me

to wipe you?"

"No! I mean no, thank you. This is horridly embarrassing!"

"Don't worry one more second about it. I've seen and done so much worse!" she laughed and handed me a washcloth.

After she left the room taking the gallon of my bodily fluids with her, I picked up the phone and called Josh.

"Hey, babe. Are you done with the spinal tap?" he asked immediately.

"Yes. And I've just had a new low..."

FIFTEEN
Friends and family

"KNOCK, KNOCK! CAN we come in?" Alexa asked.

I perked up and turned off the TV. My hand went to the hair hanging across my face and I tucked it behind my ear.

"Yes! Please," I waved my hand signaling Denise and Alexa to come in.

Alexa walked over with a balloon bouquet and flowers and set it on my bedside table.

"Hi, girl," she bent and hugged me, trying not to get tangled up in my IV and other wires that were monitoring me.

"Hey, you two. I'm so glad to see you both! Thank you for the flowers. They're beautiful!"

"We thought you could use some cheering up. Tanya is on a business trip and sends her love. The flowers are from her, too. When can you go home?" Dee asked.

"I'm not sure yet. I had a spinal tap today and they are running a few more tests."

"You had a spinal tap? That sounds horrible," Alexa said pulling a chair over so she was sitting on the left-hand side of my bed.

"It wasn't pleasant, but not as bad as I was expecting. I have to take it easy for the next week so my spinal fluid doesn't leak. What have you guys been up to? Give me the scoop."

"Well, the Warriors ended up winning Kenpo's challenge. I'm so glad that's done," Alexa explained.

"You guys were nuts to do doubles," Dee said plopping down in the chair on my right.

"I know. It was crazy. But at the time, it felt so good to be doing that. Now we all have hurt ourselves," I smiled over at Alexa.

Dee leaned closer to me and asked, "What can we be doing to help?"

"Nothing. You're helping a ton getting the kids from school. I'll pay you back."

"No, you won't. I don't care if I pick them up the rest of the year. It's no big deal."

I grinned at Dee. "Thank you. It really helps."

A quiet knock was heard on the door and Carter peeked his head in.

"Hey, guys! Come in!" I was so excited to see my kids.

Alexa and Dee stood. "We're going to take off. We'll come back tomorrow and check on you. Love you girl." Alexa gripped my hand and squeezed it.

"Thank you both for coming and for the flowers," I told them and waved.

My kids were standing sheepishly in the doorway.

"Come in, babies. Get in bed with me," I patted the sides of my bed and one by one my kids climbed in with me.

I held Carter under my right arm, Jillian on my left, and Chase snuggled at my legs.

I breathed in their sweet scents, a combination of Carter's hair gel, Jillian's shampoo, and Chase's laundry detergent smell on his shirt. They were exactly what I needed.

I grinned up at Josh, "Thank you. You all are exactly what I've been needing."

He squeezed my leg and sat down in the chair Alexa had been sitting in.

"That was sweet of the girls to bring you flowers," he gestured over to where they were sitting on the bedside table.

"It was a surprise but I loved seeing them. How was everyone's day?"

Just then the nurse walked in to take my vitals.

"Oh, do you need them to move?" I asked pointing to my kids.

"Absolutely not. That's about one of the sweetest sights I've seen with you all in that tiny bed."

"I needed to squeeze my babies tonight," I hugged them a little tighter.

The nurse took my blood pressure and recorded it on the computer.

"I love having that done," Chase said pointing to the blood pressure cuff. "It feels good."

I laughed. "You're nuts. Did you guys eat dinner yet?"

"We did. We had chicken. Chicken boobies," Jillian explained.

I smiled, "Nice. Do you guys want to go to the nourishment station and get some pop or juice?"

"Can we? I'll take them!" Chase volunteered. The three of them took off down the hallway.

"How're you holding up, hon?" Josh asked.

"I'm so glad to have that spinal tap done and get answers. It hurt and using a bed pan is not on my list of favorite things."

The kids roared back into the room and were all chatting about the drinks they got.

"Kiddos, you have to be quieter," Josh scolded.

"They're fine. Come back into bed and snuggle me," I patted the bed again and they climbed back in. We positioned the bedside table so they could put their drinks on it. I changed the channels to find a show they could watch.

"How about *Grown Ups?*" I asked. It was on the part of the movie when they're on the waterslide.

I closed my eyes for a minute and inhaled deeply. Listening to their laughter and feeling their warm bodies pressed against me relaxed me. I wanted to go home.

"OK, kiddos, we have to go home," Josh explained.

"We want to stay with Momma. I can sleep here," Carter protested.

"I would love that sweet boy, but you guys have school tomorrow. And I think I'll be able to come home tomorrow, anyway," I kissed the top of his head.

They all slowly got up and looked at me with sad eyes. I felt exactly the same way.

"Thank you for coming to see me. I'll hopefully see you at home tomorrow. Love you guys."

"We love you, Momma," Chase said.

Carter bent to give me one more hug and then Jillian laid her head on my chest.

"Good night, sweethearts," I blew them all a kiss as they walked out the door. "Bye, babe." I called to Josh. He smiled and mouthed *I love you.*

It had been a long day and I decided to go to sleep. Tomorrow was a new day.

THE SUNLIGHT POURED in through the curtains and I rubbed my eyes. It was Wednesday, the 11th of December. I was so glad that we were all done with our Christmas shopping for the kids. Otherwise, I would be really antsy to get out of this hospital room.

A new nurse whisked in and immediately I could sense her bubbliness. I smiled as she greeted me.

"Good morning! How did you sleep?" she asked.

"Pretty good. How are you?" I asked her.

"I'm great! Thanks for asking," she proceeded to write her name on the white board that hung on the opposite wall from me. "I'm Sheila. I'll be your nurse until seven tonight."

"What are the odds of me going home today?"

"It's looking pretty good. You're scheduled for an ultrasound tonight at seven. If that comes back clear, you can go home."

"Why are they doing an ultrasound?"

"I guess your last CT came back with something on your liver so they want to take a closer look."

"Of course it did..."

"Pardon?" Sheila asked.

"Oh, nothing. It seems like the more the doctors keep looking the more they find wrong with me."

She smiled. "Sometimes that happens. Breakfast will be delivered soon. I'll be back to check on you in a little while."

My room was quiet once again and I decided to get on Facebook. After scrolling through the newsfeed, I posted a picture of my balloons and flowers. My status update was "I'm so thankful for the outpouring of support I've received over the last few days in the hospital. Thank you for all the calls, texts, Facebook messages, and visits. You all have helped me to stay positive. And... I'm still in the hospital but am crossing my fingers that after one more ultrasound at 7:00 p.m. I can go home. Thank you to Denise, Alexa, and Tanya for the beautiful flowers, balloons, and most of all for your visit. <3"

I posted my update and then switched my phone off. It rang almost immediately.

"Hey, Dad," I answered.

"Hi, I bought a plane ticket and I'm coming out this afternoon. Can Josh pick me up?"

"You are?" I grinned. "That's a nice surprise! Yes, I'll have him pick you up."

"I thought I needed to get out there so I could hear more about the tests that they're doing. Mom will come out next week to help."

"Thank you, Dad. I can't wait to see you. What time will you be here?"

"I land at two. See you soon."

I hung up and texted Josh.

Me: *Hey my dad is flying in at 2. Can you pls pick him up at the airport?*

Josh: *Yes. He called me.*

Me: *Thx! Luv u!*

Josh: *See u soon. Luv u!*

I glanced up from my phone as my door opened. It was Dr. Yu.

"Hi, Dr. Yu. How are you today?"

"I'm well. How are you doing?"

"They got my spinal tap done and said I'll have the results in 72 hours. I hope to be going home today. How will I get the results?" I asked him.

"I'm scheduling you an appointment at my office on Friday.

Call my front desk girls and tell them to squeeze you in on my lunch hour. I'll have the results for you then."

"Are you sure you don't mind doing it on your lunch hour?"

"Not at all. Call them right now so you can get scheduled. And call me in the meantime if you have any questions. I'll see you on Friday."

"I will. Thank you."

Dr. Yu left my room and I quickly made an appointment for noon on Friday. I would feel better once I finally had results.

I ATE MY lunch early because you can't have any food for seven hours prior to an ultrasound. I was packing up the few items of clothes that I had pulled out in preparation to go home later than night.

"Hey, Kate, can I come in?" Alexa asked.

"Of course! How are you? It's so nice to see you."

"I had an appointment down here and thought I would stop in. Any news?"

"I have my ultrasound at seven and then I'm hoping to go home. Josh is picking up my dad at the airport and I'm expecting them anytime."

"How about now?" Dad's deep voice asked.

"Hey!" I walked over to where my dad was walking in the door. "It's so good to see you," I wrapped my arms around his belly and hugged him. "Hi, babe." I smiled at Josh.

"Dad, this is Alexa. Alexa, this is my dad, Bill."

"It's wonderful to meet you, Bill. I should go..." Alexa said.

"Nonsense. Pull up a chair," my dad instructed.

Everyone had just sat down when Sheila came into the

room holding a phone.

She handed it to me and said, "It's Dr. P. He wants to talk to you."

Alexa said, "We should leave and give you some privacy."

"No, don't worry about it. It's fine. Just give me a second," I said reaching for the phone.

"Hello?"

"Hi, Catherine. This is Dr. P. I wanted to tell you that we found something on your scan. You have a hemangioma growing on your liver with its own blood source. I've ordered an ultrasound to be done today to look at it more closely."

"OK, what will need to be done?"

"We'll have more answers after your ultrasound."

"Alright. Thank you for calling," I hung up the phone and handed it to Sheila. She was already writing the word *hemangioma* on the white board.

"What did the doctor say?" my dad asked.

I started laughing. Josh cocked his head and looked at me like I was losing my mind. Maybe I was...

"I guess I now have a hemangioma on my liver with its own blood source. They'll look more closely at it on the ultrasound. Honestly, can I have any more things wrong with me?"

"Those are common. Don't get yourself worked up just yet," Dad stated.

"They are common? Then I'm not going to worry about it until there's something to worry about." I glanced at the clock. "You guys need to go and pick up the kids from school. They'll be excited to see you, Pops."

"Call me after your ultrasound and I'll be back to pick you up tonight. I hope," Josh said.

"I *am* going home tonight. I can't stay here one more day or they'll find something else wrong with me," I chuckled. "I'll call you later. Bye, guys."

The ultrasound went fine and I would need to have a follow-up ultrasound in six months. I was released from the hospital after four days around 9 p.m. The dogs went crazy when I walked in the door. I was so glad to be home.

I bent down to pet Molly and she piddled on the floor.

"Some things never change," I smiled and sighed walking into the family room.

"Hey, Pops," I called to my dad who was watching TV on the couch. Chase walked out from his bedroom with a sleepy expression on his face.

"Hi, Momma. You're home!" He came over to me and I pulled him into a hug.

"Hey, bud! I missed you. I'm home now. You can go back to sleep. I'll be right there to tuck you in," I kissed his forehead.

I smiled at my dad and Josh and headed into the kids' rooms to check on them. They had no idea how much I missed them the last four days.

SIXTEEN

Spinal tap results

JOSH GOT THE kids to school in the morning so I could sleep in. I was weak and hurting. I still had the numbness in my legs and my head felt like it might burst. Even though I had dealt with a daily headache for so long now, I still couldn't get used to the pain.

I received a lot of texts and messages asking for an update on my condition. I decided it was easier to post a status on Facebook so more people could get instant answers. Sitting down at my computer, I quickly typed up this update before hitting post: *I'm finally home! I'm beyond excited to be back with my hubby and kiddos. It was a long four days in the hospital. So many people were asking what was wrong so here's the update... I went into the hospital on Sunday with pain and numbness from the waist down. I'd been numb for three weeks but it was getting worse. They ended up doing 5 MRIs, 2 CTs, and a spinal tap. The numbness in my legs was determined to be that I overstretched my hip flexor and damaged it. I need rest, PT, and some meds to fix that. When they scanned the brain, a large lesion was found on my right frontal lobe. I had a stroke last year and I thought that what they were finding was the old one. The neurologist said that it didn't look like an old stroke should. So they did more testing and a spinal tap to see what it could be. He is thinking a tumor, MS, or another stroke. I have an appointment with him tomorrow to get the results back to see if it's any of those things. In the meantime, I'm supposed to be taking it easy so my spinal fluid doesn't leak from the spinal tap. I greatly appreciate all of the prayers, texts, calls, and visits from everyone. When I was lying in the hospital bed, a million thoughts crept in my mind and honestly I was in a bad place. It was the constant reminders from all of you and your support that helped encourage me to stay strong. It's amazing how quickly life can change and I feel so blessed to be able to count on friends and family to help calm me and tell me it's all going to be okay. I love you all and will keep you posted as to what news I receive from the doctor tomorrow. Until then, I'm squeezing my babies a little tighter and counting the infinite number of blessings I have in my life.*

My day passed quickly as I slept through most of it. My kids got home from school and I was plunged back into our nightly routine. Dad was helping with homework and I made dinner. Josh was at a business meeting in Phoenix.

It was getting close to bedtime and I was exhausted, although I hadn't done much. I was anxious for my doctor appointment tomorrow with Dr. Yu. It would be nice to have my dad and Josh there with me.

My phone dinged signaling I had a Facebook message. I opened up my messenger and smiled when I looked down at the name— Alissa Sheldon.

Alissa was in the same grade as my brother, so three years ahead of me. I had always looked up to her as she always portrayed confidence and success in all she did. She was smart as well as beautiful and her smile lit up the room.

Her message was this, "Kate, you are such an inspiration. Hang in there and know you are in my prayers every day. Hoping for good news for you tomorrow."

I typed back a message to her, "Thank you so much! It's been a difficult journey and isn't over yet. I gain strength through all of the wonderful people in my life like you. It'll be good to get some answers tomorrow so I can move on to treatment. Thank you for reaching out! Be well!"

Alissa then responded, "I am not making this public, but I was diagnosed with breast cancer over Thanksgiving weekend and will go for surgery next Thursday. It is so awful having something so out of your control, and all I want to do is get the treatment rolling and get it behind me so I can have my life back. Seeing how you have handled your situation with such grace has helped me find the courage to handle mine. Thank you."

I was blown away that someone that I had looked up to and watched on Facebook could be struggling as I was and I didn't even know.

I quickly responded, "I'm so sorry to hear about that! Wow, it just goes to show you that you never really know what people are struggling with just by looking at them. I know that you're loved dearly and have always been a strong person. I remember looking up to you when we were in high school. You were always such an independent woman. I know that your strength will pull you through this, too. Don't be afraid to lean on people and those around you that love you.

I'm here if you ever need to talk. I've had a few moments when I've been in a dark place. When you're faced with your mortality it's easy to slip sometimes into a not so positive place. If you've felt like this just know that you're not alone.

God has big plans for you. Sometimes it's hard to understand why things like this happen to us, but I firmly believe that both of us will be okay. I've prayed for you that your surgery will be a success and that you won't have any more cancer after the surgery.

Please let me know how I can help and know that you aren't alone. Be well, my friend."

After just a few messages back and forth, we were instantly connected again. Over the course of the next year and a half and still today, Alissa remains my rock. She has beaten cancer and did it with such grace and dignity. I would rely on her and she on me in the coming months.

"Mommy, can I have a glass of juice, please?" Jillian pulled me out of my thoughts.

"Of course, sweet girl," I opened the refrigerator and while I was getting the juice out I heard the chime signaling someone had opened the door.

"Sounds like Daddy is home!" I looked into the hallway and Josh was in fact home but the bigger surprise was my sister walking toward me.

"Liz?" I was so confused for a moment. She wasn't supposed to be here and yet she was standing in my family room.

"Hey, sis. Surprise!" she laughed.

"Whaaaaat?" I questioned and looked to Josh.

"I thought you could use your sister so I flew her out on points," Josh grinned and came to my side.

"Thank you, babe!" I threw my arms around his neck and squeezed him. My eyes teared up a little and next I went to my sister. "Hi! I'm so glad you're here!" I hugged her and she held on to me tightly for a moment. My little sister had always been one of my best friends. Having her here was just what I needed.

"I'm glad to be here! Give me a job. How can I help?" Liz asked.

"You made it here just in time for bed. Can you read with Jillian? I'll take Carter."

"No problem!" Liz took Jillian off in the direction of her room.

"Chase, you have 15 more minutes, bud," I called to Chase and put my hand on Carter's shoulder leading him to his room.

MY DAD, SISTER, Josh and I were all piled in the car heading to Dr. Yu's office to get the results of the spinal tap. I was fidgeting in my seat and nervous about what he might say.

"If you guys don't mind, I want to go back by myself," I said to them.

"Whatever you want, Kater," my sister replied.

It's not that I didn't want their support. I did. It's just that I had a feeling it was MS and I needed to be able to come to terms with that diagnosis first —before having to worry about how Josh, my sister, and my dad would react.

I checked in at the front desk and realized that Dr. Yu was the only doctor in this office. There were two other people in the waiting room sitting in the chairs opposite us.

Too nervous to talk, I pulled out my phone and played *Words with Friends* with my good friend Andria. I was able to keep my mind off of my dreaded results for a short time.

"Catherine?" the nurse called my name in the doorway.

I stood and glanced nervously at Josh.

"We'll be right here when you get done," he said, and reached over and squeezed my leg.

They did the typical things at the start of the appointment—

taking my weight, blood pressure, and asking about what medicines I was on.

"Dr. Yu will be in shortly," Marissa said.

"Thank you," I nodded and watched as she left the room. My eyes wandered around looking at the different posters of the body and brain that hung on the wall.

The door opened and Dr. Yu came through it wearing a light lavender button down shirt.

"Hi, Kate. How are you today?"

"I'm good. How are you?"

"Fine. So I have the results of your spinal tap," his fingers typed over the keyboard that he had positioned on his lap.

I leaned forward slightly in my seat and wiped my sweaty palms down my thigh.

"And? What do I have? MS?" I asked nervously.

"No. The test shows no MS, although that is a difficult disease to properly diagnose."

"Oh, thank God!" I blew out the breath I had been holding. "So what do I have then?"

"I want to run one more test. I still think number one," he held up his index finger, "is a tumor. There's a test called an MRI Spec test that will evaluate the tissue of the mass. It will give us a definite answer to what the pathology of it is. It's a very expensive test and I have to get it covered by your insurance."

"OK, are you sure it's not another stroke?"

"No, it doesn't look like a stroke but that's why we need to do this test. I'll start making the calls to your insurance carrier to see if we can get it scheduled."

"Should I just wait until I hear from the imaging center then?" I asked.

"Yes, they'll call you to schedule it."

"Thank you, Dr. Yu, for everything you've already done for me."

"I'm just doing my job," he said humbly.

"No way! You've been amazing through all of this."

He pulled out his card and wrote down a number. "This is my cell number. I want you to call me anytime until we get this figured out."

Was this guy serious? I had never had health care this personal and attentive before.

I took the card from him and slipped it in my pocket.

"Alright, I will. Thank you again. I like your shirt, too," I grinned at him. "That's my favorite color."

"It's the same color you were wearing the first day I met you. I wanted to be twins," he chuckled.

I laughed. "Well, it looks good on you."

"Let's make another appointment for three weeks. That should be plenty of time to get your test done and the results back."

"Sounds good. Merry Christmas," I stood and he led me out the door to the reception area so I could make my appointment for January 6.

"Take care, Kate. See you soon. Please call if you need anything," he smiled and walked into exam room two.

I set up my appointment and then walked through the door to the waiting room. I could see the looks of concern in my family's face. Josh stood immediately and I motioned for them to all follow me outside. We stood under a tree that lined the sidewalk.

"Well? What did he say?" Josh's voice quivered as he asked me.

"I don't have MS!" The words poured out of me.

My dad blew out a noise and Josh and Liz murmured their reliefs.

"I have to have an MRI Spec test done to see if it's a tumor or a stroke, but that's fine."

"Why do you seem so relieved and not worried?" Josh asked me.

"Because no one has thought it was a tumor except for Dr. Yu and if it was another stroke, then I'm OK. I don't have any lasting effects minus these headaches. I feel so relieved! This is the best news I could've gotten. Let's go eat. I'm starving." I started walking toward the car.

I caught the glance my dad gave my sister but it couldn't take me out of the sense of relief I was feeling. I was going to be all right.

We went to lunch at an Italian place in downtown Chandler. I had pasta and devoured it like I hadn't eaten in days. My stomach had been tied in knots since the hospital and I finally felt as though things were looking up.

My dad brought up the mass again at lunch and stated that he still didn't think a stroke and its qualities fit me. I casually brushed it off and told him the test would tell us definitively what it was. Until then, I was taking this news as not having MS as a small victory. Sometimes, though, victories—no matter how big or small—can be very short lived.

SEVENTEEN

The results that would forever change me.

MY MOM HAD flown in for Christmas and my dad had gone home a few weeks before. He's a pilot and flew himself back down on Christmas Eve. We picked him up at the small airport that was just five minutes from my house.

The 24th, I had my urologist appointment in the afternoon. The doctor went up through my urethra and viewed my bladder to see about the thickening of the wall.

That test had been uncomfortable but another health issue was checked off the list that day. My bladder looked healthy and not thick anymore. He thought that possibly my bladder wall had become inflamed when I overstretched my hip flexor and caused it injury. I was given a clean bill of health and no bladder cancer for me.

We were able to enjoy Christmas at home as it was the first time we've ever been home on the actual day. We always split our holiday and would spend part of the time in Iowa visiting my family and part of the time in Wisconsin visiting Josh's parents.

My mom cooked all the meals and I smiled as I watched my kids' faces light up at whatever gifts they were opening. I cherished every second of laughter, smiles, and the joy I felt that Christmas. My greatest gifts hadn't been wrapped in a box that year... they were the blessings that were all around me; my kids, my parents, Josh. I was alive and feeling hopeful for the first time in a long time. I would heal and my nerves would regenerate. I forced myself to believe that I was getting better.

I went down to St. Joseph's hospital on the 27th and had my MRI Spec test done. It took a while longer that I had expected. I had been waiting almost an hour and there was only one other person in the room waiting on a test.

"Excuse me, ma'am? I was just wondering how much longer before my MRI?" I asked at the reception desk.

"It shouldn't be too much longer, dear. We had a slight insurance issue. The normal MRI was approved but not the other special portion. Your doctor has actually been on the phone with your insurance company for the last 20 minutes and just now got it approved. It won't be much longer now," she explained as she looked over her blue glasses.

"OK, thank you."

"Just have a seat."

I walked back over to where I had been sitting and shook my head. Dr. Yu is amazing. That was the only word to describe this doctor that kept going to bat for me time and time again. He knew I needed that MRI Spec test to find out what the mass was. A regular MRI wouldn't show us the pathology of the tissue as I had already had multiple MRIs. What neurologist had 20 minutes to personally talk to my insurance company? He didn't have the time—Dr. Yu *made* the time. And essentially saved my life again by refusing to give up when the insurance company wouldn't do the test.

The MRI Spec test took about two hours to complete. It was done on Friday, December 27 in the afternoon. I wondered how long it would take before I would get my results.

The New Year came and went without much craziness. We usually spent New Year's Eve doing something with the kids. For Christmas, I had given Josh tickets to see the Criss Angel magic show in Vegas. We were leaving on January 3 and taking the kids with us.

Las Vegas is a short five-hour drive for us and one of Josh's favorite places. It would be the perfect weekend trip to getaway and use Josh's Christmas gift.

It was Thursday, January 2 and I realized that I still hadn't gotten my test results back. I had gone to see Randy in the afternoon and walked out to my car when PT was over.

I decided that I would call Dr. Yu's office and see if they had gotten the results.

"Hi, this is Kate Mathias. I'm just calling to see if Dr. Yu has gotten the results of my MRI Spec test yet?"

"Hi, hmm, it doesn't look like we have them yet but with the 1st falling mid-week, their offices may have been closed for a few days."

"Do you think it would help if I called and checked with them?"

"Absolutely. If they have them, go ahead and have them fax the results to us. I see you have an appointment on Monday with Dr. Yu. If there is anything that shows up on the test, he will call you today. Otherwise, he'll wait for your appointment on Monday," the woman told me.

"That works. I'll call them right now," I said and hung up the phone.

I was sitting in my car in the parking lot of physical therapy building and punched into Google to search for the number for St.

Joseph's hospital. I found the number and hit *call*.

A woman answered right away. "Hello, St. Joseph's Hospital, Imaging Center."

"Hi, I was wondering if you could help me to find some test results?" I asked.

"Sure. Name?" she asked.

"Catherine Mathias."

"Birthdate, Catherine?"

"2-14-77."

"It looks like I have the results of the MRI Spec test right here. Should I send them over to you?"

"Actually, can you fax them to my doctor's office? Dr. Kan Yu."

"I'll do it right now. I have his information in your chart."

"Thank you. I appreciate that."

I'm glad I called. Who knows how long they've been sitting on someone's desk.

I called Dr. Yu's office back again.

"Hi, it's Kate Mathias again. They are supposed to be sending you over my results. Can you please let me know if you don't receive them?"

"Of course, and remember that he won't call you unless there's something to report."

"That's fine. Thank you." I hung up the phone and started my car. It was time for me to pick up the kids from school.

"BUT WHY DO we have to do them, Mom? They don't even help," Carter pleaded with me as we drove to get the boys' allergy shots.

"I know that you don't think they help, but they do, honey. You used to sniff all of the time. We only have about another year and we'll be done with them. Did you guys bring your homework?" I asked the kids as I quickly changed lanes so I could turn into the parking lot.

"I don't have any," Carter told me.

"I just have some math. It won't take me long," Chase said.

"I don't have any either, Momma," Jillian piped up.

I pulled alongside the curb and threw the gearshift in park. "Run in and get your name down. I'll park and be right there," I instructed the boys.

Driving down a few spaces, I pulled in and parked under a tree.

"Let's go, sweet girl," I opened Jillian's door and hit my clicker to lock the doors. I smiled as she skipped on ahead of me holding her pink iPad case.

We had to do shots once a month. They called the boys back and Chase got three shots and Carter would get two. Chase never really complained, but Carter would come out with ice packs on both arms. He's usually my high pain tolerance kid but the shots bothered him for some reason.

I pulled open the door and Jillian immediately went back to get a sticker. We were all used to the routine. I spotted the boys sitting along the back wall.

"Hey. Did you get your names in?" I asked them taking a seat next to Carter.

"I did. I'm almost finished with my math," Chase scribbled down some answers. "Then let's play, Carter." He and Carter brought their iPods and would play while we waited for shots.

"Chase. Carter," a woman's voice paged over the intercom.

"Can you hold this please?" Carter handed me his iPod and then followed his brother back.

They were gone about one minute and came back to sit next to me. I smiled at Carter as he held the ice packs on his arms.

"Did it burn, bud?"

"Yeah, it hurt," his face grimaced. "Chase, are you ready to play?"

My cell phone started vibrating in my hand. I looked down at the number and my mouth went instantly dry. It was Dr. Yu's office.

"Chase, watch your siblings please. I'll be right back," I jumped up and walked the 10 feet to the one stall private bathroom and turned the handle. Luckily, it was vacant. Closing the door behind me I pushed *accept* on my phone.

"Hello?" I half whispered.

"Hello, Kate? Can you talk?" Dr. Yu asked.

"Yes, sorry. I'm at the doctor's office but I can talk. Did you find something on the test?"

"Actually yes, they did find something. You have a low-grade glioma brain tumor," he stated.

"What?" I surely didn't hear that correctly. "I have a brain tumor?"

"Yes, that's what the results show."

"No way," the words came out of my mouth but I was having trouble comprehending what he was saying.

"I thought it looked like a tumor all along."

"Yes, you did say that, but wow... a brain tumor. What do we do now, Dr. Yu?"

I have a brain tumor. Brain tumor.

"You have an appointment on Monday. I'll recommend a neurosurgeon at either Mayo or Barrow for you to consult with. Do you have any questions for me?"

I have a million questions. Why me? Would I die? Would I see my children grow up?

"I have no idea. I'm sorry. I'm in shock right now," I squeaked out.

"It's understandable. It's a positive thing that it's low-grade. You'll know more after you speak with the surgeon on your options. Do you still have my number if you have questions and need to call over the weekend?"

"Yes. I have it. Thank you," my hand holding the phone started to shake and my other hand reached up to swipe away a tear that escaped my lashes without me knowing it.

"I'll see you on Monday," Dr. Yu's calm voice reached down into the darkness that I was already plummeting into.

"OK, bye," I said, absentmindedly, hanging up the phone. I dropped my phone in my purse and placed both palms down on the cool stone counter. I looked at my reflection in the mirror. My eyes looked hollow and I had dark circles underneath them. I looked sick.

I inhaled deeply. I needed to put on a brave face for my kids. I needed to get us all home safely before I could freak out.

The words *brain tumor* echoed in my head and they didn't feel real. How could I have had a brain tumor all of this time and not known it?

My hand grasped the cold door handle and I pulled open the door. I walked over and sat down next to Carter again. My whole body was quivering.

Chase glanced up at me, "Mom, what's wrong? Was that the doctor?"

I clamped my shaky hand between my knees to hide my fear from my kids.

"It was. They wanted to remind me about my appointment Monday. I'm fine, babe."

Liar.

Would I ever be "fine" again?

"Mom, you're shaking. What's wrong?" Chase asked again.

Carter and Jillian then stopped what they were doing to look at me.

"Carter. Chase," the woman paged the boys again, saving me.

"C'mon Carter," Chase motioned with his hand to his little brother to go back to have their arms checked.

I blew out the breath I had been holding. Jillian climbed up on my lap. I smiled down at her and then wrapped my arms around her small frame. I squeezed her and drew strength from my tiny super girl.

I would fight this with all I had in me. I had to—for my kids.

PULLING INTO THE garage, I've never felt more grateful to have driven home safely. The neighbor kids were outside playing and I could hardly pull the car in the garage before my children were throwing their doors open.

"Can we play?" Jillian asked.

"For just a few minutes. It's almost dinnertime. I have to run in and tell Daddy something and then I'll be back out," I waved to Shayla and Kris. "I'll be right back out. I just need to tell Josh something," I called to them pointing my index finger up to show them one minute.

Shayla waved and grinned.

Josh had gotten home from a business trip while we were at shots. I could hear the shower running as I opened the door from the garage. He often showered after traveling all day on the plane.

I had almost removed myself from my diagnosis. I felt detached and that I was thinking about someone else's life... someone else's tumor.

The shower door was open and the steam was pouring out into the bathroom.

"Hey, babe. How were shots?" Josh questioned me, soaping up his hair.

"Hi. Dr. Yu called while I was there."

"What did he say?"

"I have a brain tumor."

That's it. Exactly how I said it. No sugar coating. No softening of the words. Just the facts.

I watched as Josh's face changed and his eyes clouded with worry. His hands dropped from his head to his sides. The warm water pelted his back and was the only noise I heard.

"OK," Josh was at a loss for words.

"We have an appointment with Dr. Yu on Monday. Can you come with me?"

"Of course. I don't leave until Tuesday for my trip. What else did he say? A tumor? It's really a tumor?" Josh said, stunned.

I shrugged. "I guess so. The test showed it's a low-grade glioma. I really don't know more than that."

"We can't leave for Vegas tomorrow. Not after getting this news..."

"Yes, we can and we are. What difference does it make if we are here or in Vegas? It doesn't change the fact that I have a brain tumor. Besides, it'll help to take my mind off things. Otherwise I would just sit around stewing about it."

"Whatever you want to do, babe. I just want to support you," Josh reached out and held my arm. "Let me dry off so I can hold you."

"It's fine. The kids are outside. I'm gonna go tell Kris and

Shayla and then we'll be in."

"Whatever you need to do. And Kater, I love you," his lips curved into a sad grin.

"I love you. I'll be right back."

I walked outside and Kris and Shayla were talking at the bottom of their driveway. The kids were racing around on their bikes and laughing.

"Hey, girl," Shayla called as I walked up.

"Hey. I just found out that I have a brain tumor."

Again, I just blurted it out. It still sounded foreign to me and felt as though I was telling them about someone else.

"My God." Shayla immediately walked over to where I was standing and gave me a big hug.

"Really? I wouldn't have guessed that. You didn't have any of the common symptoms except for the headache," Kris said.

"I guess they think it's a low-grade glioma. I have an appointment with my neurologist on Monday to get a recommendation for a neurosurgeon."

"Barrow is the absolute best place to go for something like this. They'll take good care of you," Kris explained.

"You think I should go there instead of Mayo?" I asked.

"They're world renowned. They've operated on kings and queens. People from all over the world come to Barrow for surgery."

"OK, then that's where I should go," I stated.

I looked over to where Denise was walking down the sidewalk.

"Hey. What's going on?" she smiled at the three of us.

Shayla looked to me and then answered, "Not a lot. What're you up to?"

"Oh, you know, been busy with work."

"I just found out the results from my test. It wasn't a stroke. I have a brain tumor," I stated calmly.

Denise didn't say a word. She just walked over to me and pulled me into her arms. I held on tightly to her.

"It's fine. I'll be fine."

"Whatever I can do to help with the kids, let me know."

"Thank you. I may need your help carpooling."

"Whatever you need. No problem," she replied.

"Do you guys mind watching the kids for a minute? I need to go in and call my parents." No sooner had I said that I heard the door slam and Josh walked out.

I turned and waved to my neighbors—my friends.

"See ya later." I walked toward Josh. "Hon, I'm going to go in and call my folks. Can you please watch the kids?"

"Sure, Bear. You doin' OK?" He slid his hand down my arm.

I just nodded and headed in to make some calls.

I called my brother first. The conversation went the same as it had with Josh. He asked questions and I told Bill all that I knew at the time. He was calm. Actually, I was calm. I could tell people without crying as though it wasn't really happening.

The call to my parents was the same as Bill. I promised to keep them posted on how I was feeling and my appointment on Monday.

After I hung up with my parents, I sent my brother a text.

Me: *Hey can you call Mom and talk to her? She's freaked out and I don't think I did a great job assuring her. It's all too much for me right now.*

Bill: *Of course. Call me with any questions.*

Me: *I will. Thx Bill.*

I needed to let friends and the rest of my family know about the tumor so I sent out a blanket text.

Me: *Hey all. I got my results back from the MRI Spec test. It showed I have a brain tumor. They think it's a low-grade glioma. I go to see my neurologist on Monday. He'll refer me to a neurosurgeon. Will keep you posted.*

I paused a moment before I hit send. This would go out to my sister, cousins, Josh's parents and brother, and my friends. I shrugged my shoulders to myself and tapped the button to send it.

About 30 seconds passed before my sister was calling.

"Hello?"

"Seriously? You can't just send a message saying you have a brain tumor," she said.

"Sorry. It's just... just... I don't know. Weird. I thought it was easier than having to keep talking about it."

"I get that, but my gosh! How are you doing?"

"It's hard to explain. I guess I'm in the denial stage. It doesn't really feel like it's happening to me."

"What's the next step?"

"I have an appointment on Monday with my neurologist. I'll keep you posted."

"Should I fly out there?"

"Thanks sis, but let's wait until we know more. I may need your help if I have to have surgery," I explained.

"What did Bill say?"

"He had questions but I don't have a lot of answers right now."

"I'm gonna call him," Liz said.

"That sounds good. I'm going to let you go. I need to go make dinner and I'm tired."

"I love you, sister. Call me tomorrow," Liz said.

"OK. I love you, too. Bye," I hung up the phone. Immediately, my phone started pinging with text messages from friends and family.

I would answer one and another would come right back in. Maybe I should've rethought my telling approach. I answered them all with the same thing stating, that I would know more next week after my appointment with Dr. Yu.

I slipped my phone in my pocket and trudged out to the kitchen. Josh was already standing at the sink washing some fruit.

"Hey. I just came out to get dinner ready."

"You look tired. Why don't you go lie down and I'll call you when it's ready?"

"You don't mind?" I asked him.

"Not at all. Go rest," he shooed me away with his hand.

I walked back to our bedroom and plopped down on the bed. Molly immediately jumped up and curled her small body around my stomach. I fell asleep stroking her head.

EIGHTEEN

Vegas, Baby!

"EVERYONE READY?" I looked back at my kids in the back of my SUV.

"Ready!" Jillian shouted.

"I'm ready to see those guys with the cards on the sidewalk," Chase said with a devilish grin.

"No, you and your brother aren't to touch those or even look at them," I smiled and shook my head. I caught Josh's look out of the corner of my eye. He was smiling and chuckled.

"How long's the drive?" Carter asked.

"About five and a half hours. Do you want me to put on a movie for you?"

"Yeah, Tom and Jerry please," Carter handed me up a DVD from the pile that I had brought.

I loved that the kids still liked Tom and Jerry. I used to watch that cartoon when I was a kid. Once the kids were watching the movie and not paying attention to us, Josh reached over and intertwined his fingers in mine.

"How are you feeling, babe?"

I motioned to be quiet by putting my finger to my lips. Chase listened to everything we talked about. Often times I would forget that he was there and he would bring up topics later when he wasn't supposed to be a part of the original conversation.

"I'm fine. My head hurts pretty badly today. Do you mind if I take a nap?"

"Go ahead. Get some sleep."

We pulled into the Cosmo a short five hours later. It was a Marriott property, so when I booked it I had used Josh's hotel points so we could stay for free. Just one of the perks of having him travel all the time. It felt weird to be standing in the lobby of a Vegas hotel with our kids. We were *that* family.

Our room was nice and overlooked the Bellagio fountain. Josh took the kids out on the balcony to see the twinkling lights that were just starting to light up the night.

"Be careful. Don't go out too far. It makes me nervous," I called from inside the room.

"They're fine. Hey guys, turn around so I can get your picture," Josh instructed them.

I watched as they turned around and smiled big for the camera. I think I was trying to memorize every single line on their faces.

How many more moments like these would I have left?

"Alright, kiddos, come in and get changed. We have to leave for dinner in a few minutes," I started pulling out their clothes and laid them on the bed.

I stood upright slowly and sighed.

"You OK?" Josh came over to where I was standing next to the bed.

"I'm OK, just tired. I don't think I can walk to dinner tonight. Do you think we can take a taxi?"

"Sure. You mean you don't want to walk like last time?" he laughed.

I swatted at him with my hand and grinned at him. Looking out the window I said to him, "I can almost see the Hard Rock from here."

"Who would've ever made you walk that far?" Laughing, he turned to Carter, "Let me fix your hair, bud."

I had taken Josh to Vegas for his 21st birthday and he had a grand plan that we could walk to dinner because we could see the Hard Rock from our window. It turned out that it was four miles one way... through dirt... in heels. I would never let him forget that bad decision.

We were eating at Joe's Stone Crab restaurant and it was one of our favorite places to go. There are only three of them in the country and we have been to all three.

We had a great meal and then walked around briefly at Caesar's Forum shops. We made a last minute decision to go see the Cirque du Soleil show, 'O'. The kids watched in amazement at all of the activity that filled the stage and spilled out to where we were sitting as the performers swung above our heads.

Hundreds of people filed out of the auditorium. I gripped the handrail and slowly walked down the steps.

"I can't walk anymore. Can you piggy back me?" I asked Josh.

He cocked his eyebrow and looked at me to see if I was serious.

"I'm not that serious... kinda," I laughed. "Let's go back to the hotel and to bed."

We slowly walked back through Caesar's Palace hotel and popped out on the sidewalk. The men with the cards of the naked ladies were in full card-slapping force.

"Don't even make eye contact. Keep on walking, boys." I put my hand on Chase's shoulder and rushed him along at a quicker pace.

"What're those cards Daddy? Can I see one?" Jillian looked up at Josh, her hand placed firmly in his.

"They're not cards for you to look at. C'mon. We're almost there," he explained and looked over his shoulder at me. "You doing alright, Kater?"

"Yeah, I'm good," I answered back and then squinted my eyes as I looked at Carter.

He had caught one of those cards under his shoe and was dragging it along the sidewalk. Pulling his leg slowly behind him as not to lose the card, he bend down and reached for it.

"Nice try, dude. Keep on walking!" I scolded him.

"Aww, Carter! You almost got away with it!" Chase laughed and slapped his hand on his little brother's back.

"You don't need to look at those for a few more years, bud." I smiled at him and grabbed his hand leading him into the lobby of our hotel.

THE NEXT DAY we spent going to the Candy Factory and to the aquarium. I was losing steam but slowly trudged on behind the kids as we looked at the sharks swimming in the tanks.

The sunlight bounced off the water and created shimmering shadows of light that danced on the walls. I smiled to myself watching the kids' amazement as they stared at all of the colorful fish.

"Let's go grab lunch. I'm starving," I said and we walked out into the food court area.

"I want a hot dog, Daddy," Jillian said.

"The boys and I will have cheeseburgers from Johnny Rockets.

I'm going to sit here and hold this table down," I patted my hand on the table.

"Chase, come with me and help me carry the food please," Josh instructed, and he and Chase went off in the direction of the food.

"What was your favorite part of today?" I asked the kids.

"I liked seeing the turtles!" Carter exclaimed.

"I know you love turtles," I grinned at him.

"Can we get one, Momma?"

"We'll see. Not right now but maybe when I feel better." I turned to Jillian, "What was your favorite part of the day, sweet girl?"

"I really liked all of the jellyfish. I'm soooo hungry!" Jillian sighed.

"I am, too. Here comes Dad and Chase with the food," I pointed.

"Here we go!" Josh placed the tray on the table and started passing out the food.

We inhaled the burgers and the hot dogs and then decided to walk through the Wynn. We ran into our friends Jason and Sommer in the lobby.

We had only talked to them for just a few minutes when Jillian tugged on my shirt.

"Momma, I don't feel well," she whispered to me.

"OK, you're probably tired," I told her. I gave Sommer and Jason a quick hug and rushed her outside to stand in the taxi line.

"We'll go back to the hotel and rest before we head to the show," Josh said.

"Momma, I'm going to throw up," Jillian leaned over and lost her lunch on the sidewalk in the taxi line.

I moved quickly and grabbed her hair, pulling it back and reached around her waist to steady her. She didn't get any on us and wiped her mouth off on her arm when she was finished.

"I feel better," she smiled and looked up at me.

Josh laughed, "I know you're not the first girl to puke in the taxi line at the Wynn."

We got her a bottle of water and got her back up to the room. She lay down on the bed but seemed to be instantly better.

"Why don't we all get a shower and get cleaned up before the show starts?"

THE CRISS ANGEL magic show was in the Luxor. We walked through the lobby of the pyramid-shape hotel and made our way to where the double doors were open, leading into the concession area.

"Check out all of these cool motorcycles. They all have different names," I pointed to the real motorcycles that were housed behind glassed-in cases. There had to be about 10 of them lining the edges of the hallway to the theater.

"Let's get some popcorn for the show," Josh suggested and we moved slowly into the large line that had already formed for the food.

We were going to go to dinner after the show so it would be good to have something to tide us over until we could eat.

Holding our two tubs of popcorn and balancing our drinks, we walked into the small theater and toward our seats, which were in the center and weren't too far back. I didn't know what to expect out of this show but looked forward to it.

The show started with Criss floating down from the top of the stage. They had bits of humor in the show, some of it adult jokes, but Chase got most of them and laughed hysterically right along with Josh and me.

I watched the kids' faces; they were just as awestruck as I was at the illusions he was doing. At one point, Criss asked the audience if we were enjoying the show because no one was clapping. We were all so amazed at the tricks that the audience was forgetting to clap!

The show seemed to rush by in a blur and we spent the evening switching between laughing and being astonished about the illusions Criss Angel was pulling off. I knew that the last trick had to be getting close as the show was almost over.

"For my last illusion I'm going to be doing something that if you're queasy about blood you may want to look away," Criss explained. "One woman in the front row didn't believe me during my last show and ended up passing out."

I looked at Josh and mouthed, "Are you going to be all right?"

He smiled and nodded.

I watched with curiosity as they wheeled out a large wooden table to the middle of the stage. Next out was the largest table saw I've ever seen. Its diameter had to be about six feet across.

Carter leaned over to me, "What're they going to do with that?"

"Good question. Let's watch," I said, pointing to where his assistant was walking across the stage.

"My assistant will climb on the table. I need someone to come up and make sure that her restraints are real and solid," he explained to the audience. People raised their hands. "OK, madam, you in the red shirt. Please come up here."

The assistant was lying on her back with both hands and legs restrained. I've seen this trick done before but always with a box that covered the body, so when she was cut in half they could have one person in each box. How was he going to do this trick with her completely in the open?

We anxiously watched as the woman in the red shirt pulled on the restraints and nodded.

"You agree that they are indeed real?" Criss asked her.

"Yes, I confirm," she spoke into the microphone and then walked off the stage.

"OK then. Fire it up!" Criss instructed.

The giant saw started spinning and picked up speed. The buzzing noise filled the otherwise quiet room. Everyone was holding their breath. Another assistant in a white lab coat lowered the saw— cutting the woman in half.

Sparks were flying as the blade cut through the table and hit the floor. Blood literally flew off the stage and splattered on anything and anyone that was near. Gasps were heard throughout the room. No one could believe their eyes.

My hand flew up to my mouth. I looked over at Josh whose jaw was hanging open.

My eyes snapped back to the stage and I watched as an assistant pulled the top half of the table off one side of the stage while another wheeled the bottom half of the table and half of the woman off the other side.

"Unbelievable..." I whispered.

"Is she dead?" Carter leaned over and croaked at me.

"No, it's all just an illusion. But that was a really good one!" I explained clapping my hands, still stunned.

"Thank you for being with us tonight. If you have a camera, go ahead and pull it out. Tweet to me about the show. Thank you all for coming. Until next time!" Criss Angel smiled and waved.

I quickly pulled out my phone and clicked a quick picture of him on the stage. When the show started they had told us that pictures were forbidden.

The lights came up in the auditorium and people began making their way out to the lobby.

All of the kids started talking at once.

"Did she really die?" Jillian asked.

"How did he do that?" Carter muttered.

"That was awesome when all the blood sprayed all over. I thought Dad was going to lose it!" Chase laughed.

I put my hand on Carter's shoulder and glided him out behind Josh.

"That was an awesome show! Did you like it?" I asked Josh.

"It was so good! Let's go grab dinner and we can talk more about it there," Josh said and led the way out of the lobby to the main doors of the hotel.

We made our way back to Caesar's Palace and decided to eat at an Italian place. Everywhere else had a big line and they could get us right in. It was close to nine o'clock and the kids were all tired. *I* was tired.

Jillian started whining slightly that she was so sleepy that she couldn't eat.

"We'll order something fast and then go to bed," Josh explained, picking up his menu. "What're you doing, Kater?"

"I'm tweeting to Criss Angel."

"What does that mean?" Chase asked.

"I joined Twitter awhile back for my author stuff. I'm attaching the picture I took of Criss Angel and then saying something quick about his show."

Chase leaned over so he could watch what I was doing.

"So I just click right here and then I can type a status. Let's see... I'm gonna put ***@CrissAngel My kids are still talking about whether or not your assistant died in that trick. Unbelievable!! Wow!*** Then I'm going to add the picture right here. And hit tweet and it's done!" I put my phone down on the table and looked up as the waitress come over to take our order.

Josh ordered salad and spaghetti for the table.

My phone beeped and buzzed. Then again. It started chiming and vibrating.

"What the heck?" I picked up my phone and looked at the notifications.

"Is everything alright, bear?" Josh asked.

I looked down at the phone. "Unreal."

"What?" Chase asked.

"Criss Angel just retweeted my tweet to 969,127 followers."

"What does that mean?"

"It means that he liked my tweet and basically just reposted it again for the people that follow him. Look at this!" I held my phone up for Josh to see. "People are favoriting it and retweeting it again. This is crazy!"

My phone kept beeping so much that I had to turn it to silence as it was annoying everyone around us.

"That's so cool, Mom. You're famous!" Chase said excitedly.

I laughed. "I don't know about that but it is pretty cool that he did that. Only took him 13 minutes since the time I posted it, too. I'm sure whoever manages his page did it, but still."

I picked up a piece of bread and dipped it in oil. "Someone responded to my tweet that she's seen the show six times and the assistant doesn't really die. It looked so real!" I said to the kids. "I wonder how he did that?"

I would continue to get that tweet favorited or retweeted for the next six months. It would always make me smile when a notification would pop up on my phone saying someone else liked my status. It reminded me of a carefree time with my family, which would be in short supply in the next few months.

NINETEEN
My visit with my neurosurgeon

ON OUR DRIVE home from Vegas, we stopped at the airport and picked up my mother-in-law, who would be staying with us for the next week. As she got in the car, the kids were excitedly telling her about our weekend.

We pulled into the garage and everyone grabbed a bag out of the trunk and dumped it in the laundry room. I would be washing clothes for the next few days trying to get everything caught back up.

"Hey, everyone: Head in and shower. I'll bring your jammies," I called as the kids raced into our room with the dogs nipping at their heels.

"How can I help?" Suzi asked.

"I think we're good. You can go unpack and we'll meet you out in the family room in a bit. Do *you* need anything?" I responded.

"Nope. I'm just happy to be here." She smiled at me and began pulling her rolling suitcase down the tile hallway.

I sighed.

"Babe, I'll get the kids showered. Why don't you go sit down? You look tired," Josh squeezed my arm.

"I *am* tired but I'll get their jammies and be right back," I smiled weakly at him and walked through the house flipping on lights as I walked in each room.

I noticed the answering machine was flashing a '1' as I made my way through the kitchen. I pressed the button and listened as a woman's voice came on.

"Catherine, this is a call to remind you of your upcoming appointment with Dr. Yu at two o'clock on Monday the 6th. Please call the office to reschedule if this appointment will no longer work for you."

Taking a deep breath, I was quickly brought back into reality. In all honesty, the words "brain tumor" echoed in my head every few seconds the entire weekend but I tried to pretend that this really wasn't happening to me. I rested my elbows on the counter and lowered my face into my hands. My head was pounding.

I heard Suzi walk up behind me. I lifted my head.

"Did you get settled?"

"I did. Can I read with the kids before bed?" she asked.

"They would love that," I said. "I have my neurologist appointment tomorrow. Do you mind hanging out here while Josh and I go so you can be home when the kids get back from school?"

"Sure. Whatever I can do to help."

"Thanks. I need to go grab their jammies and then we'll start getting them to bed."

JOSH REACHED OVER and squeezed my leg. I curved the edges of my lips upward, not showing any teeth.

We were back in Dr. Yu's office and I didn't really know what to expect. I was so glad that Josh was here with me. My knee bounced up and down absentmindedly.

Pressing my palms down, I rubbed the sweat that had left a thin film on my hands onto my jeans. The door opened with no noise and Dr. Yu came walking in.

"Hi, Kate. How are you doing today?" Dr. Yu asked, rolling the black chair over a little closer to us and taking a seat.

"Hey, Dr. Yu. Do you remember my husband, Josh?" I asked.

"Nice to see you Dr. Yu," Josh reached out and shook his hand.

Dr. Yu nodded, smiled and flipped open his laptop. "Well, Kate. So it *was* a tumor." He smiled.

"I know... I honestly can't believe it. And you were the only one that thought so. You saved me. I can't thank you enough," my eyes watered slightly and I swallowed.

"It was nothing," he waved his hand humbly. "Now, would you like to go to Mayo Clinic or Barrow? I'll recommend a neurosurgeon at either place."

I looked at Josh. "I think we want to go to Barrow."

"OK. Good choice," his fingers swiftly stroked the keys.

"What will they do?" Josh asked. "Will they do a biopsy?"

"Yes. They'll go in and cut out the tumor. Remove it."

I gasped.

"What?" I asked. "You mean the whole thing? I don't know why but I was thinking they would just take a small sample like other biopsies I've had," I reached for Josh's hand and held on tightly to his fingers.

"To get a sample they still have to cut through the skull so they might as well remove it completely," Dr. Yu said.

"That actually makes a lot of sense," Josh stated.

"What will that mean for me long term when that portion of my brain is gone?" I asked.

"The frontal lobe controls the executive decision-making skills, memory, judgment, some coordination, and your social filter. It may not affect you at all or you may have lasting effects. It's truly hard to say how you'll respond."

"But I could be different after surgery?" I nearly whispered.

"Of course."

"Will she still be as stubborn as she is now?" Josh tried to make light of the situation.

"Yes. She's stubborn so she can put up with you..." he laughed.

Josh and I both chuckled. This is just another way that Dr. Yu is amazing—he always tries to make me feel safe and not threatened.

"I'll have my front desk girls make you an appointment with Barrow's. They'll call you to get that scheduled. I'll be sure that all of your files are transferred right over to them."

I nodded.

"That's it? No other questions?" he asked.

"Not that I can think of right now. Thank you," I stood and gave him a hug.

"Anytime. I'll see you soon, Kate. Take care." He left the room.

Josh and I walked out into the cool day. Unlocking the car doors, Josh opened my door for me and I climbed into the front seat.

As Josh began the 20 minute drive home I studied his profile. He wasn't talking. And neither was I.

Tears started to well in my eyes and I quickly swiped at them trying to catch them before they fell.

What if I'm mean to my kids after? What if Josh doesn't like me anymore?

Horrible thoughts swirled around in my head threatening to take over.

"Katers? What are you thinking?" Josh broke the silence.

"All of this time, I've been worrying that I'm going to die *in* the surgery. What if who I am dies instead? What if I'm mean? What if you don't like me? What if *I* don't like me? What if—" The words poured out of me, threatening to choke me.

"We could worry about the what-ifs all day, but I think we try and take this one day at a time," he said. "I'm guessing that we'll know more after we talk to the neurosurgeon. Would you feel better if you called your brother?"

I nodded and pulled out my phone. He would be just finishing with work.

I inhaled deeply while I waited for the phone to connect. He answered on the third ring.

"Hey, Kate! How did your appointment go?"

"Fine. He said that they'd remove the whole tumor. I don't know why, but that surprised me. I'm nervous," I explained.

"Did he tell you how the surgery would be done?"

"A little bit. They're making me an appointment with a neurosurgeon at Barrow. I guess I'll find out more after talking with him. Bill, am I going to be different?" I asked.

"There was a guy that had a brain tumor the size of an orange when I went to medical school. His personality is the same. He had to go through radiation and chemo though and it killed his pituitary gland. He's pretty tired all the time now. Did the doctor say you would have to do chemo and radiation?"

"I don't know. Didn't ask. I'll ask at the other appointment. Do you think my personality will change? He said it affects executive decision-making skills, judgment, and filter."

"You could have some personality changes but probably you

won't be like Jekyll and Hyde or anything," he said.

"That's what worries me the most. I don't want to change and be mean to my kids or Josh."

"I wouldn't worry about that now. You won't know what will happen until after the surgery."

"OK, thanks, brother. I'll let you know when they get the appointment scheduled with Barrow's."

"That sounds good. Talk to you soon. Keep hanging in there, Kater."

I nodded.

"I'm trying. Bye, Bill," I clicked off the phone and looked at Josh.

He reached over and placed his hand on my leg.

"No matter what, Bear, we're gonna get through this, you know."

"I hope so." I squeezed his hand and rested my head back on the seat.

BARROW NEUROLOGICAL INSTITUTE called on Tuesday that week and scheduled an appointment with Dr. S on Thursday of the same week. Josh left to go out of town on Tuesday after we met with Dr. Yu. He was flying home on Thursday and would meet me at the appointment. It was scheduled for 4:30 p.m. and happened to be not too far from the airport. Suzi, would stay home and watch the kids after school.

Barrow was about 40 minutes from my house, but I left an hour early so I would have plenty of time. Traffic can get heavy during that time of the day.

I pulled into the parking garage and turned up the first lane. I happened to see Josh's white car parking in a spot on the right. I drove past him and parked a few spots up. He hadn't gotten out of his car yet.

I wandered down to where he was still sitting in the car and noticed he was on the phone. I opened the passenger side and slid into the seat next to him.

"That'll work. Let me put some numbers together and I'll shoot you an e-mail later tonight. No problem. Yes. That's fine. OK, talk to you later," he said, depressing the end button on his Blackberry.

"Hey, babe. Did you have any problems finding it? How are you holding up?" he asked.

I shrugged my shoulders.

"Good. I'm tired. I'm anxious to hear what this doctor has to say. Bill sent me a list of questions to ask him," I waved a piece of white paper before tucking it in my purse.

"That was nice of him. And it'll be helpful. Are you ready to go in?

"I guess. I feel sick to my stomach," I clutched my belly and pushed open the door. Josh and I walked hand in hand down the parking garage toward the light where the street was. We needed to cross the street and the office was on the main floor.

As the doors slid open automatically I was surprised at how many people were there—all ages of people young and old. My eyebrow rose unintentionally as an older woman walked by. Half of her hair was shaved and she had a long, crooked scar that ran the length of her skull from front to back.

Josh noticed her, too. He pulled me faster towards the check-in desk.

"Is that what I'm going to look like?" I whispered to him.

"Maybe, but at least you'll be alive."

Good point.

"Hi. Catherine Mathias checking in," I told the lady at the front desk.

"Hello, Catherine. Can you please fill out these forms and then return them to me with your ID and insurance card?"

I smiled and took the clipboard. Sitting down in the orange chairs, I quickly scribbled through the paperwork while Josh worked on his Blackberry. They were all the same except this time I had to mark the box for brain tumor/brain cancer.

I pointed that box out to Josh with my pen, and he pressed his lips together in a thin line and nodded.

"Catherine?" a nurse called my name.

"Hi, that's me. And you can call me Kate. I'm not quite done with these forms."

"No problem. Come with me and you can finish them in the back."

"OK," I followed her and said, "This is my husband, Josh." We walked a short distance to a room and she instructed us to take a seat.

"I'm Diane. I'm Dr. S's nurse. Let's get a quick weight check and blood pressure."

I slipped off my shoes and climbed on the scale. The numbers flickered and stopped on 128. I was losing weight and pretty quickly, too.

"Dr. S is the best. I've been working with him for 16 years. He'll be in shortly."

I had Googled Dr. S before we came to the appointment and knew that he was older. He had performed over 4,000 Gamma Knife procedures. The Gamma Knife was cutting edge, literally, in brain surgeries.

Unfolding my questions from Bill, I smoothed them on my leg

and waited. Josh was in deep thought. He didn't speak but just sat on my right-hand side.

Dr. S walked in and introduced himself, closing the wooden door behind him.

He sat down in the chair across from us and held a clipboard. His fingers flipped through the pages of what I assumed was my chart and was quiet for a moment.

"So tell me about all of *this*," he motioned to the papers in his lap.

I quickly told my story about the neurologist thinking I had a stroke and up until the time where I met Dr. Yu and found out about the brain tumor. He used a pencil to jot down notes as I spoke. Asking specific questions about my health, it took about 30 minutes or so to catch him up on what was going on healthwise with me. Then it was my turn to ask him questions.

"How will this go?" I asked.

Turning in his chair so he could face me straight on he answered, "Our tumor board meets on Monday mornings. I'll present your case to them and we'll determine if we think surgery is a viable option."

"Do you vote on it or how do you decide?" Josh asked.

"We don't necessarily have a formal vote. It's a board of 10 to 15 neurosurgeons that'll evaluate your case based on the location of the tumor, size, and accessibility."

"OK, then assuming that the board thinks it's a good idea for me to have surgery, what happens next?" I asked.

"We'll set up surgery and do an MRI right before. We use a live MRI machine during surgery and it's very exact. There will be a few surgeons in the operating room with me. We'll make a small, approximately 2 inches, window-size hole in your skull and go in and remove the tumor. Then we'll reattach your skull using titanium strips and close up your scalp." He shifted his body weight in his chair.

He continued, "A frozen section is biopsied immediately and we'll find out what type of tumor we're dealing with. A permanent test will be done and it usually takes about 72 hours to get results. You'll be in the ICU for a few days, depending on how surgery goes," Dr. S explained.

"What about chemo or radiation?" Josh asked.

"It's too early to discuss those options yet. We need to see what type of tumor we're dealing with," Dr. S said.

"And what if the tumor comes back?" I asked.

"Then we either do spot radiation on it or remove it again, but we can discuss those options at a later date if necessary."

I swallowed the lump that had formed in my throat. Turning to Josh, I nodded.

"OK, thank you doctor. Now do I just wait to hear from you?" I asked.

"Yes, I'll call you after the tumor board meets on Monday. It starts at eight o'clock and usually lasts just a few hours. Does Diane have a good number to reach you?"

As if by magic, Diane walked through the door. I smiled as I saw her and realized that they had done this numerous times.

"Yes—Kate, is your cell phone the best number for Dr. S to reach you?"

"That's fine. Thank you," I stood and reached for Dr. S's hand to shake it.

Josh did the same, and Dr. S collected his papers.

"I'll be in touch," he left the room and took all of my air with him.

I gulped in a deep breath and looked at Diane and Josh with teary eyes.

"You're in good hands... the best," she said. "We'll wait to hear from Dr. S and go from there. You can exit down the hall and to your right. Have a good night," Diane smiled and pulled the door shut behind her.

IT WAS MONDAY, January 13th and Chase had his celebration of learning at school at 1:30 p.m. Josh was out of town, and Chase really wanted me to videotape the celebration because he made it on the Principal's List Honor Roll for getting all As.

Getting the kids ready for school that day was a blur. I kept checking the time and then would ask myself if the doctors were still meeting?

I had a few minutes before I needed to leave for the school and the text alert sound on my phone went off.

Josh: *Heard anything yet?*

Me: *No. I'll call u as soon as he calls me. Getting ready to go to Chase's thing. Luv u!*

Josh: *Luv u!*

As soon as I put my phone down it rang and my mom's face lit up the screen.

"Hi, Mom!" I answered.

"Oh, honey, just wanted to see if you had heard anything yet?"

"Nothing yet Mom. I'm expecting him to call anytime, though. Hey, I'm just getting ready to go to school for Chase's celebration of learning. Can I call you back later?" I asked.

"Sure, honey. I'm just very anxious," Mom sighed.

"I know. I am, too. Call you later."

I clicked the phone off and slipped it in my pocket. I quickly put the dogs in my room and turned on the security alarm. It immediately began beeping and counting down as I closed the door.

"Please don't let me miss Chase's thing..." I prayed out loud, hoping that the doctor would call me after his celebration.

I hopped in the car and shut the garage door. The drive to the school was quick and I scanned the parking lot looking for a space.

Smiling, I got out of the car and looked around at all of the parents that were able to come and support their children. Multiple moms and dads were milling into the school headed for the multipurpose room.

I walked into the already-crowded gym and saw my friend Shatha wave. I waved back and took a seat near the back where one was available.

My phone lay dark and silent on my lap. I hit the home button for the 20th time to check the time and to see if I'd missed *the* call.

The celebration was starting and I had trouble sitting still.

Please let me get through Chase's thing... please.

The words tumbled around in my head as I caught Chase's eye and gave him the thumbs up sign and smiled. When it came time for his name to be called, I videoed him walking proudly up on stage and shaking the principal's hand.

"Go, Chase!" I yelled out and clapped with one hand against my jeans while holding my phone still to capture his moment.

I had made it. I didn't miss this *and* managed to video it for Josh.

Chase mouthed *thank you* to me and I smiled. I nodded and mouthed back, *I love you.* The celebration was over and the doctor hadn't called. It was close to 2:15 p.m. and I was starting to wonder and worry.

Denise, Shatha, and Sandy walked over to me as the kids were filing out of the gym and heading back to their classrooms.

"Hey, girl," I said as I hugged Sandy.

"Any news yet?" she asked. Sandy is one of Chase's friend's mom and my good friend, too.

"Has the doctor called yet?" Denise asked about the same time.

"No. Not yet. He should be calling anytime, though," I clutched the phone tighter in my palm willing it to ring.

"Don't worry. I'm sure he'll call soon," Shatha reassured me quietly.

"I hope so. Congrats to all your kiddos. They're awesome—" I started to say when I felt my hand start to vibrate.

"Oh, God. It's him," I whispered as I stared down at the screen and panicked just a little.

"Go! Answer it!" Denise prodded me.

It was still loud in the gym with all of the parents there so I took off running for the exit doors out to the playground. It had already rang three times and I didn't want to miss him.

Pushing open the door a little too roughly, it swung back and hit the wall pouring me into the cool outside. I was where the kids ate lunch and luckily no one was on the playground. It was quiet and still.

I quickly slid my finger over the phone to answer the call and spoke breathlessly, "Hello?"

"Kate? This is Dr. S calling."

"Yes, hi, Dr. S. How are you?" I asked him as I walked a few feet to the picnic table that sat under some shade structures. My heart was pounding and I willed it to slow down.

"I'm fine. We met with the tumor board today and I have some things to discuss with you. Do you have a moment?"

"Yes. Please go ahead," I croaked out trying to breathe and hold my breath at the same time.

"The group doesn't necessarily vote per se on the cases. I presented yours and it was unanimous that we all think you should have the tumor removed."

"OK."

"That being said, you do have options. We can wait and watch it for six months and then do another MRI, or we can schedule surgery. My colleagues thought that since it appears to have grown in the last year and with its location that you're a good candidate for surgery. We aren't certain that it has indeed grown or how much as there *is* some human error because a different technician ran the tests. Its location is on the surface of the brain, which is good as it doesn't look embedded. Why don't you discuss this with your husband and let me know how you want to proceed?" Dr. S explained.

"Honestly, I've talked *ad nauseum* with my husband about what we would do if you came back and suggested surgery. In just these few days since we met with you, all I can think about is the tumor. I don't think that I can wait six more months knowing that I have a tumor in my brain. I would constantly be wondering if it was growing or if my headache was really bad one day if something was happening to it. So... I think I want to go ahead and schedule the surgery."

"Understood. I'll have Diane check the schedule and call you tomorrow. If you have any questions for me in the meantime, please don't hesitate to call my office."

"Thank you, Dr. S. I will. Bye." I clicked off my phone and stared down at it.

I was going to have brain surgery to have a brain tumor removed.

Brain surgery.

It didn't feel real. This wasn't really happening to me.

A text flashed across my screen.

Sandy: *Are you still on campus?*

Me: *Yes, I'll come around the front.*

I walked the few hundred feet to the front of the building and saw my three friends standing in the grass looking for me.

"Hey," I called to them.

"Oh, my gosh! You *are* still here! We didn't know if you took the call and left. What did the doctor say?" Sandy asked.

"The tumor board says I need to have it removed. They'll call me to schedule surgery," I explained. It was easy to say those words. I felt like I was talking about someone else. "I feel better knowing now. Is that weird? I'm relieved, actually."

"No, it's not weird. Sometimes it's a relief to get answers," Denise said.

"What can we do to help?" Shatha asked.

"Thank you. I may need help with the kids around surgery time but don't know when that is. I'll keep you posted, if that's cool?"

"Sure. Just let us know," Sandy said and pulled me into a hug.

"I haven't even told Josh yet. I'm going to go call him and get in line to pick up the kids. I talk to you all later," I waved and headed in the direction of my car.

I plopped into the cool comfort of my car and pushed Josh's number to call. I heard rustling as he answered.

"Babe? Hey, what did the doctor say?" Josh asked.

"Hi, am I catching you in the middle of a meeting?"

"I stepped out. It's okay. What did the doctor say?" he asked again.

"I have to have surgery. All of the doctors decided unanimously that it should be removed. Yeah, so..."

"Okaaaaay. Wow."

"I know," I whispered. "I actually feel relieved a little. It's strange."

"I think you are because now we actually know. We'll get through this together. I love you, Katers."

"I love you, too. I see the kids running up so I'm going to get off. Should we tell them when you get home on Thursday night? I should know when surgery is scheduled by then."

"I think that sounds like a good plan. Call you later tonight," Josh said.

"Sounds good, babe. Bye," I punched the button to disconnect the phone just as the kids were pulling open the doors.

"Hey, guys! How was your day?" I asked smiling at my kiddos, the three lights of my life. I pulled away from the curb and headed toward home wondering if during the next few weeks I would be wondering if this would be one of my last times to pick up my kids from school or maybe one of my last times to do anything.

TWENTY

The month leading up to my brain surgery

AFTER A RESTLESS night's sleep, I woke and got the kids off to school. To my kids, all was the same in their eyes. They had no idea that my entire world had been shaken like a snow globe and set back down leaving me feeling rattled and unstable.

I hadn't cried when I called my parents and family. I sent out a mass text message and told people that I had to have surgery to have the tumor removed. That moment I hit send, I already felt disconnected to what laid ahead of me.

The honest truth was I couldn't wrap my head around the fact that I not only had a brain tumor but also had to have it removed. It wasn't really real. It wasn't really happening to me.

I was sitting at my writing desk and just staring off in the distance when my phone rang. I recognized the number and immediately answered it.

"Hello?"

"Hi, Kate? This is Diane with Barrow."

"Hi, Diane. How are you today?"

"I'm good. How are you holding up?"

"I'm actually doing okay. Did you get a date for surgery set?" I asked her.

"Yes, that's why I'm calling. I apologize that it's taken so long. You have to have another test run to see if your speech is located on your right side of your brain and there's only one machine in Phoenix. It's all booked up for three weeks so we've scheduled your surgery for February 11. You'll have your pre-surgical appointment and test on that Friday before. I'll send you all of the paperwork in the mail so you know where to go."

"That sounds good," I had flipped open my computer and was mentally looking at the four weeks I would have before surgery. "Can I ask you a couple of questions that I thought of?"

"Sure, ask away," she replied.

"My birthday is on the 14th. Do you think I'll be out of the hospital by then?"

"That'll really depend on how the surgery goes. But as long as you're recovering well, they like to send you home as soon as possible. People get sick in hospitals and you're healthy otherwise, right?" she asked.

"Yes, I am. I mean besides the tumor."

"Then maybe you'll be home. We'll do our best."

"OK, also can you tell me about the incision? How much hair will I lose?"

"That all depends, too, on how they have to go in to remove it. You may have about a 4 by 6 inch shaved section of your hair. The doctors are very careful, though, and sometimes I can't even tell where people's incisions are unless they show me. I know that with your beautiful hair it's a worry, but the doctors are very cognizant of trying to not make a mess of your hair," she said, and I could hear the smile in her voice.

"Thank you. I think that's all I had to ask you."

"No problem. Feel free to call if you think of any other questions. Please watch for the paperwork. We'll need to have you sign the forms and mail them back to us to get it all in the system for insurance."

"I'll send them right back when I get them. Thanks again," I told her.

"You're welcome. Have a good afternoon!"

I pushed end on my call and sent a text to Josh knowing he was in a meeting.

Me: *Hey surgery is set for Feb 11ᵗʰ. Happy bday to me!*

Josh: *Wow. Ok. It'll be good to get it done. Luv u! Call you in a few.*

Me: *Luv u!*

JOSH GOT HOME from his business trip on Thursday night. We decided to tell the kids about the tumor since we knew when the surgery was set. I served up dinner and was pouring the milk.

"Kiddos! Time to eat!" I called to them.

Josh came into the kitchen. "Can I help with anything?"

"Can you put the milk on the table please?" I walked past him and set the two plates I was carrying down in front of Jillian and Carter.

"Chase, can you please pass the salt?" Jillian asked.

"No snow mountains like last time, sister," I warned her.

"I know. I just need a little salt," she grinned up at me with her cheeky smile.

I looked over at Josh and he nodded. It was time.

"So Dad and I want to tell you something. You know how I've been sick and have headaches every day?" I watched their heads nod. "Well, Mommy found out that I have a brain tumor and have to have surgery to have it removed."

I paused for a moment and then continued, "I know this is really scary and both Dad and I are worried, too. We hope though that as soon as they remove the tumor, I'll feel good again. What questions do you have?"

Chase looked over at me with serious eyes, "Is this fatal?"

He was 10 but had always been very mature for his age. His question didn't surprise me but how he worded it did. He was very concise and factual and that is exactly how I would answer him.

"We aren't sure yet, Chase. It can be fatal. Even if the tumor is benign—meaning it's not cancerous—it can still kill me because your brain is only so big. When a tumor is growing in there, it's pressing on vital parts that can cause death if it gets too big or compresses on the brain just right."

Josh reached over and took my hand, squeezing it. "Mom has the best doctors that will be doing the surgery and we hope for the best."

Chase swallowed and nodded his head. His hand was still grasping his fork but he wasn't eating.

I looked at Carter and Jillian. Carter spoke next and shyly asked, "How long do you have to be in the hospital again?"

"I'm not sure, baby. Maybe a week?" I told him. "Try not to worry. Gigi Carolyn will be here and Daddy will bring you down to see me this time." Carter was concerned because last time I was in the hospital he didn't see me until after I had been gone for three nights. He was only 8, and me not being home when I usually was, was his biggest concern.

I turned to Jillian. "Do you have any questions, sweet girl?"

"No, Mommy," she looked up at me and then reached for her glass for a drink. She and Carter thankfully didn't understand the severity of the situation. And I would protect them from it as long as I could.

WHEN WE HAD gotten the surgery date set, my cousin Jeff had called to say that he and his wife, Kerri, wanted to come out to visit me before the operation. I was grateful for the distraction. Kerri came in on Sunday and Jeff would come later on Wednesday that week.

On Tuesday the 21st, Kerri and I were out laying by my pool and Josh had come out to talk to us on his lunch break.

"This sun feels so good," I murmured to Kerri. My head was killing me but I had already taken a lot of pain medicine and couldn't take anymore. We were out soaking up some rays before I had to get the kids from school.

"So this is what you do all day, huh?" Josh teased.

I smiled at him and retorted, "You're just jealous that—" I was interrupted when my phone rang. "It's Dr. S's office," I spoke out loud seeing the caller I.D.

"Answer it!" Josh said.

"Hello?"

"Hi, Kate. It's Diane from Barrow. I'm calling to check to see if we can move your surgery up to Monday, the tenth instead of the eleventh?"

"Hmm. Sure. That's fine," I said.

"Great. There will be three surgeons in the operating room and one of them was having problems with his schedule and wants to be in on your surgery. I'll e-mail out a new check-in time so you'll have it, but surgery is now set for 10:30 a.m. with a check-in time of 8:30 a.m. I have you scheduled for your pre-op appointment and MRI speech test on Friday the seventh at 11:30 a.m."

"I'll be there. Thank you for calling," I told Diane.

"Sure. Thank you for switching."

I hung up and my eyes filled with tears.

"What's wrong, babe?"

"They changed my surgery to Monday instead of Tuesday."

"Why?" Kerri asked.

"Something about one of the surgeon's schedules," I turned to Josh. "All of my family is coming in on Sunday. I wanted to have Monday to go to lunch with everyone and you know... have one last hoorah." With my hand, I wiped away a tear that had dropped on my cheek.

"You don't need one last hoorah, babe. You'll have plenty of time with your family after surgery. Maybe this is a good thing," Josh said.

"How is it a good thing?" I asked.

"Because maybe then you'll be home on your birthday," he smiled.

"Big whoop. I'll be in bed and in pain. What a great birthday," I muttered feeling sorry for myself.

"You don't know how you'll feel," Kerri reached over and took my hand.

I looked up at Josh and could tell he was worried about me and was only trying to help.

"I'm sorry. You're right. This is OK. At least all of my family gets in on Sunday so they can be here for the surgery," I said.

"That's true, babe. And we'll all be by your side," Josh bent to give me a quick kiss. "I have to head back in to work now. Are you OK?"

I nodded. "I'm fine. See you in a while."

WE HAD A nice visit with Jeff and Kerri and when I pulled up to the airport to drop them off, Jeff pulled me into a hug and said into my ear, "This isn't good-bye, you know."

My chest heaved and tears filled my eyes. He and I are very similar and often think the same, sometimes even saying the identical things at the same time. Kerri always said that we could be siblings instead of cousins. He was saying out loud what I was thinking.

"You don't know that," I whispered.

"Yes, I do. Now go kick that tumor's ass and be strong. Love you cuz," he released me and smiled down at me.

I hugged Kerri next and waved as they pulled their bags through the doors. I climbed back into my car and my body shook with sobs. This week I had shifted from totally detached to feeling like every single thing I did was for the last time. I was angry one minute and questioned why this was happening. The next moment, I was scared and crying... begging God to let me live.

I managed to drive home from the airport that day somehow seeing through my tears, as I couldn't stop them from falling. I couldn't stop the horrible thoughts that swirled through my mind threatening to drown me, beating me down until I couldn't get up. I was trying to fight through the darkness but couldn't seem to find the light.

My mom flew in the next day on the 27ᵗʰ. She said that she needed to be here with me to make sure I was all right.

When I picked her up from the airport she hugged me tightly and exclaimed, "You're so thin!"

I was down to 125 pounds and every one of my ribs stuck out from my sides.

"I know, Momma. I can't help it. Nothing stays in," I would eat but everything came out, even if I only drank water.

Mom took over everything from the laundry, to cooking the meals, to helping do the homework with the kids. Which was all a blessing—especially the doing the homework part.

"Honey! Where are you?" my mom called from the hallway.

"In my room, Mom," I called as I bent down to tie my shoe.

"Oh. Are you feeling OK?" She came into my bathroom and had a worried look on her face.

I laughed, "I'm fine. If I leave your sight for more than two minutes, it doesn't mean that I'm sick or something is wrong."

"No, I know. I'm just worried. Are you sure you're OK to drive to lunch today?"

My friends Shatha, Denise, and Sandy were taking me out to lunch for an early birthday celebration. I was grateful for the distraction.

"I'm good. I won't be gone too long. Are you sure you don't want to come with me?"

"No, honey. You need this time with your friends. I'm going to go on a walk and make some cookies while you're gone. Take your time."

"Bye, Momma. See you later then," I walked out the door and climbed into my car to drive to the new lunch place.

We sat on the patio and it was a cool, sunny day. The

conversation turned to our children as we all had kids in fifth grade. No one was talking about my upcoming surgery although I could tell that they wanted to ask.

"OK, so I have something to give you," Denise said when there was a lull in the conversation. She pulled out a blue book from a gift bag and handed it to me.

"What's this?" I asked taking the large book in my hands.

"Ignore the cheesy couple on the cover," Denise waved her hand dismissing the stock photo of the people smiling up at me.

I laughed and opened the front page. There was a note from Denise.

"You don't have to read it now. Just wait till you get home. I wanted to do something for you that you could read and know what people think about you."

I started reading her letter and immediately my eyes welled with tears. I couldn't do this now. I couldn't be so raw in front of my friends. I reminded myself to be strong for them—I could fake it until I felt strong for *me*.

I closed the book and held it to my chest. "Thank you," I nodded and wiped at a tear. "Thank you for doing this. Thank you for taking the time to put this together. I can't wait to read it," I said to Denise and grinned.

"It was my pleasure. I hope you enjoy it." Denise smiled back at me.

"Well girls, this has been fun but we need to scoot and go get the kids," Sandy remarked.

I glanced at my watch. "It is that time, huh? Thank you all so much for meeting me for lunch."

"Just let us know how we can help in the next few weeks," Shatha told me as she hugged me.

"I will. See you all soon." I walked to my car clutching my book to my chest.

I cranked the engine and flipped off the radio. I sat in the silence and started to read Denise's letter on the first page of my book.

Dearest Kate,

What you are about to embark on is something quite unique. It is not a new project to me; I have done this before. However, I am not the original creator of the project. But I know a good idea when I see it, and I know the power of this project. It touches everyone involved, beyond any words I can put in a letter. It will hit you at the core of your emotions. You will be overwhelmed, as I was during the making of this project.

This idea was just going to be something five or six or us were going to partake in, but you know me, I live by the "Go Big or Go Home" mindset. So, with the help of your loving husband, Josh, we were able to get this message out to quite a few people and allow them to participate as well. And they were more than willing!

In the following pages, your closest relatives and friends have taken some time to write down their feelings about you. What you mean to them, and how you have touched their lives. I wanted you to have this no matter what the outcome of your surgery may be. I wanted your kids to always have great memories of who their mother is, and they can share it with their children when they are older. But before you move on, I want to share my thoughts with you and some of your great qualities.

You moved into the neighborhood before us. Shortly after we moved in, you needed mayo. You asked for it the day I found out my dad died. I laughed when Jovan told me the neighbors, who we didn't know, needed mayo. You gave me laughter when I needed it most. I knew I'd liked you.

Before we had our pool, you always had us at yours. You always open your house to my family. You are always willing to share.

We are both middle children—that is a bond in itself we will always share.

Our kids have grown up like siblings. I hope they continue to be like that over the years. You are a mom to more than just your three. You've got my two in your corner, too.

Our texts!!! What more is there to say about those? Sheer ridiculousness.

You pulled me out of a physical rut, which was causing some mental anguish for me personally. You dragged me to the gym, and it changed my life. You were so instrumental in my physical changes and mental changes. How on earth can I ever repay you for that?

The love you and Josh share is obvious for everyone to see. It's something I hope your children strive for when they become adults and find someone to love.

I have never heard you say you hate someone or don't like them. I think that's amazing, and shows just how big your heart is and your willingness to accept everyone for who they are.

Your children are amazing in their own ways, but each of them has your spunk and quick-wittedness. That's a great quality to have. It will keep people on their toes around them.

I could go on, but many others have a lot to say. In the upcoming months, know that we are here for you.

Take some time today and enjoy this book (which will be coming in Shutterfly form) with your family.

God bless you today, and in the days and months to come. Big things are in store for you, like The Ellen Show, so you HAVE to get through this!

Love,

Denise

I took a deep breath and smiled as a tear rolled down onto the laminated page. Thank goodness that perfect letter was protected!

As I flipped through the letters I was overwhelmed just like Denise said I would be. I pulled strength from each of those letters that day as I sat in the parking lot and would again on numerous occasions when I needed to be reminded that I *could* do this.

Closing the book, I dried my tears and glanced at the clock. I only had a few minutes before Denise would be dropping off my kids from school. I had a couple of things to get at Target and thought I'd whip in there quickly before I headed home.

I KEPT MY Target shopping experience to a minimum and pulled into the garage just a few minutes after the kids had gotten home. I pushed open the door and the dogs greeted me.

"Hello!" I called from the doorway. "How is everybody?"

Carrying all of the plastic Target bags hooked through my arms, I waddled into the kitchen. I refused to make multiple trips. I dumped the bags on the counter.

"What's all this?" Mom asked, starting to unload the bags.

"Oh, I just needed to get a few things and it turned into way more like usual," I grinned and pulled out some hats.

"What're those for Mommy?" Jillian asked. The kids were all sitting at the kitchen table eating a snack.

"Well, some of my hair will be shaved for the surgery and I thought I could wear these hats until my hair grows back." I plopped on one of the hats and modeled it for them. "Do you like it?"

"You look like a robber," Carter told me.

"They should call me a robber," Chase explained, "because I steal ladies' hearts."

"Oh, boy..." I looked at my mom and we both started laughing. The kids went back to watching TV and eating their snacks.

"How was lunch?" Mom asked.

"It was great to see the girls. Denise made me this book," I tapped my finger lightly on it.

"What is it?" Mom has always been nosy and immediately started to open it.

I closed it and lifted it off the counter. "I'm not quite ready to share it yet. It's the book where my family and friends wrote to me."

"That's fine, honey. I was wondering if you had gotten it," she smiled at me.

"She gave it to me today. Thank you for your sweet note, Momma," I said with a smile.

"I meant every word," she said. She hugged me. "Now should we get homework started before dinner?"

"Yes, *you* should. I have a headache." I chuckled to myself and started to unload the rest of the Target stuff.

TWENTY-ONE

Amy

IN THE DAYS that followed that next week, I slipped further into darkness. My friend Alissa told me that I was grieving the loss of my health. It was true. I had moved from denial to anger to questioning 'why'. I was now in the stage of depression and sadness.

I've always been a positive person seeing the bright side of everything. When someone would tell me that they were sad or depressed, I didn't get it. I would think to myself to "get yourself out of it" or just "get happy". I had no idea that depression is an illness—one that you sometimes can't dig yourself out of.

I had to stop all of my pain meds and Ibuprofen 10 days prior to the surgery. I woke up daily with so much pain that some days I would dry heave from the nausea. My vision would go black if I got up too quickly. I was losing weight quickly and my body felt frail and weak.

It was February 5th and I had five days left before surgery. I had five days left.

Five days left to live.

On that Wednesday when I woke up and opened the curtains, I was greeted by a cloudy, overcast day. These types of days are rare in Arizona, as we have sunshine nearly every day. I usually look forward to the cloudy days so I can throw on a sweatshirt and feel comfy even if it's still 100 degrees out.

The day matched my mood. I looked to the heavens and wondered if the clouds were reflecting my soul.

I stepped outside and looked up at the sky for a long time. I am a Christian but was a Christer. A Christer is a Christmas/Easter churchgoer rolled into one. I would go to church on Christmas and Easter for sure. The other Sundays just didn't seem to happen. I prayed often and felt that I lived a good life, a Christian life. I didn't feel like I needed to go to church to prove that.

But today, I was struggling. I had a pang in the pit of my stomach that wasn't a physical pain, but it wouldn't go away no matter how much I begged God to save me... to give me another chance at life. Had I done something wrong to deserve this? What was the purpose of my brain tumor?

What was the purpose of me?

"Show me a sign, Lord. Any sign. Please," I begged out loud outside for affirmation that I would have more than five days left here. More time to watch my kids grow. More time to spend with Josh and my family. More time to love.

I waited. I waited for a full three minutes and nothing. Nothing came. And so feeling defeated, I opened my car door and slunk into the seat. My hope was fading.

I drove to Target for the last time before my surgery. I always get my kids Valentine's cards and a few small gifts for Valentine's Day, which also happens to be my birthday. I wanted to have them all ready to go since I might still be in the hospital on Friday, which was the 14th.

I slowly pushed my cart around the card aisles searching for the most perfect cards for my family. I decided that I wanted to have a card for my kids and Josh for each day I was in the hospital. Little love notes that they could read from me.

Standing in a sea of pink and red hearts and flowers, I plucked a card off the shelf. It read, "For my daughter..." I don't know what it said on the inside because I never made it to the middle to read it.

My daughter. My Jillian. Would I be around to shop for prom dresses with her? To teach her to drive a manual stick shift? To teach her how to follow her dreams and go after them?

I spent the better part of the next hour picking out the *perfect* cards for each of my children, Josh, and my family. My stack was quite large as I loaded them on top of the candy and other small trinkets I had found for the kids.

As I moved toward the checkout lanes, I eyed a few that were empty with no customers. But I was drawn to go to aisle five where a woman with short dark hair and glasses was just finishing ringing up a man.

I quietly unloaded my cart and was withdrawn in my own thoughts when I heard, "How are you today?"

I glanced up to see the cashier was addressing me, which I thought was kind of odd since she hadn't finished with the man yet.

"I'm good. How are you?" I asked her.

"Great! I'll be with you in just a moment," she responded.

I nodded and continued to unload my items onto the belt. The man paid and grabbed his bag, leaving the small counter.

Setting my purse on the now vacant shelf I waited as the cashier started ringing up my items.

"You have a lot of cards," she said.

I smiled, "Yes. Good cards are hard to find."

"Do you have any big plans for the weekend?" she asked.

This question caught me a little off guard. It was only Wednesday and most people didn't ask what you were going to be doing three days away. I wasn't in a habit of telling complete strangers about my brain tumor but felt compelled to share my story with her.

"Well, actually I have a brain tumor. I have surgery on Monday morning so I bought all of these cards," I turned my hand palm side up and pointed with my index finger, "so my kids would have one to open every day I'm in the hospital."

"Oh, my gosh! I'm so sorry to hear that. My friend's three-year-old daughter has cancer and I've seen what it's done to their family. I'm trying to be there to help her in any way I can. Do you have your family to support you?" she asked while she scanned my items.

I gulped and started to get choked up.

"I do. I don't think I would be making it through this without them and my friends. I'm sure you're a big help to your friend. Just being there for her means more to her than you know," I told her and smiled.

She had finished scanning my items and my total rang up to $111.53, which was a pretty tame amount for me at Target. I glanced up at her name tag, which read 'Amy'.

Amy pulled out her phone and asked, "Do you have Cartwheel?"

"No, I don't," I shook my head.

She scanned her phone and it took $1.20 off.

"Oh, thank you. Every little bit helps!" I said to her, pulling out my credit card to pay.

"Wait just a moment before you run your card," she told me.

I looked over and she was holding a red Target gift card in her hand. She scanned it and I heard a beep. I looked down at my new total and it was now $10.33. Amy had scanned a hundred dollar gift card. It wasn't one that she got off the shelf and had to put the money on like usual when you get a gift card. It was already loaded with a hundred dollars.

Confused and overwhelmed I exclaimed, "I can't accept that!"

"You can and you will. Just as I know that you're going to be OK after the surgery and be there for your kids."

I started to cry, as did she. Amy stepped around her counter and took me in her arms. I held on tightly to my angel and cried onto her shoulder. No one came up behind me to check out. For those few minutes, it was just the two of us. As my tears fell wrapped in the arms of a perfect stranger, I knew that I had indeed met the *perfect* stranger.

When I finally pulled back from her and looked into her eyes she whispered, "I'll be praying for you on Monday morning at 10:30 a.m."

I nodded and gushed, "Thank you. Thank you again... for everything."

Had I told her the time of my surgery?

I pushed my cart to the exit doors in a daze and overwhelmed by my encounter. As the doors opened automatically and I moved outside, a ray of sunshine hit me in the face. Sunlight had broken through that gloomy day.

And that's when I knew. That's when I got my sign that I *was* going to be OK. I had begged for signs since I had been diagnosed and must've been too wrapped up in my own head worrying that I missed them. He knew what I needed or rather *who* I needed. God sent me Amy that day to hold me in her arms and physically tell me that I *was* going to be OK.

I loaded my bags into the trunk and climbed into the driver side. I was filled with a sense of peace; a sense of stillness and understanding. Calmness washed over me about the struggles I had ahead. I knew in that moment that I would definitely have more moments in my life... more moments where I would make a difference in a complete stranger's life, moments where I could teach my children about the importance of love, kindness, and giving without wanting anything in return.

It was no accident that I met Amy that day and that she showed me love and compassion when I needed it the most.

I don't remember the short drive home. I was flooded with raw emotion. It filled my body and soul and reached down through the darkness that I had been trapped in. I had a new perspective on my surgery.

I would *live*.

I would fight and be here for my kids. I pulled into my garage and was standing with the trunk of my car open when my mom came rushing out.

"Oh, honey! Are you OK? You've been gone for so long. I was just about to call you," my mom asked worriedly.

"I just had the most amazing experience, Momma. I think I met an angel today. I'm not even sure she was real. I don't know if I went back to Target now if she would still be there," I chewed on my bottom lip in thought.

My mom cocked her head and lifted an eyebrow. "What happened at Target?"

"It was simply amazing. Life altering." I described Amy and my experience and my mom took in everything I was telling her. "I'm going to be OK Mom. I'm gonna make it through this surgery." I hugged my mom tightly.

"You need to share this story and post it on Facebook," she said. "People need to hear about this. Your story can give people hope."

"I think you're right. Do you mind getting the kids and I'll go post it?"

"Sure. Go do it now and I'll bring in your Target stuff," she suggested.

Logging on to Facebook, I quickly typed my experience so I could share it with my friends and family. My story ended up being 'shared' 11 times. I had often wondered why I got a brain tumor. What was the purpose? It was on that day that I think I received my answer.

The old saying goes that God doesn't give you more than you can handle and if He brings you to it, He'll bring you through it. I now believe in that but it's so much more for me. After the responses I received from spreading my Amy experience I think that really I was supposed to remind people to hope. Here's the thing about hope: Even in my darkest days, hope was always there for me. Hope for a future with my kids and husband, hope for my health to return, and hope to remember that life is filled with moments.

Lately, I'd been too bogged down with darkness to enjoy my moments, to appreciate what I had in my life, in my kids and in Josh. I think that sometimes God has things happen to you so that other people can see how you respond to a life-changing struggle. I *hoped* that I could strengthen people's faith in Him or just faith in each other.

I WAS STILL reflecting on this experience when Alexa and Tanya picked me up later that night to go to dinner to celebrate my birthday. As we drove to the restaurant, I shared in person what had happened to me today.

"I'm OK now. Truly and honestly. I think that I'm going to make it through. No. I know it," I said, determined as I spoke to my two best friends over the desserts sitting in front of me. I couldn't decide on which one so we got two. I was always a fan of dessert!

The candles flickered on top of the small cakes served in glass bowls, drizzled with caramel sauce. The small lights glimmered in the tears that formed in my eyes.

"Make a wish, girl," Tanya told me. She reached over and squeezed my hand.

I closed my eyes for a moment and took a deep breath. I blew out my candles that night and neither of my girls needed to ask me what I had wished for.

TWENTY-TWO
Three days and counting

TANYA AND ALEXA had insisted on taking me to my pre-op appointment, which consisted of my MRI scan and speech test. It was supposed to last four hours. Josh was out of town and so my mom needed to be home to pick up the kids from school.

Alexa dropped me off in the semicircle drive. "You go on in and we'll park and find you," she instructed.

I climbed out of the car and walked into St. Joseph Hospital where Barrow Neurological Institute is physically connected. Following the signs to the check-in, I gave my name to the front desk.

"Good morning. I'm Catherine Mathias checking in."

"Yes, Catherine. I have your chart right here. I see that you're scheduled for Monday at 10:30 a.m. for surgery. Check-in at 8:30 a.m.," the receptionist said.

"That's correct."

"This is where you'll check in on Monday morning," she pointed her finger down.

"OK. Thank you." I glanced around at the area with its light green walls and watched as nurses went rushing by.

"Do you have anyone with you today, dear?" she asked.

"Yes, I do. Tanya and Alexa. They're parking."

"I'll put them on the list. Follow me, please," she said, leading me to the left and down a hallway.

There were multiple rooms that were sectioned off with curtains. Each had a hospital bed and a few chairs. Some of the rooms had people lying in the beds and some were vacant.

"Go ahead and take a seat and start filling out this information. Sally will be right in to start your paperwork."

I nodded and sat down. I glanced at the clipboard filled with the paperwork I had already filled out and sent in a few weeks earlier.

"Hello, Catherine. I'm Sally and I'll be going over your pre-op information with you today."

"Hi. It's nice to meet you. And you can call me Kate."

"If that's your preferred name, I'll make a note in your file. I see that you have already started looking through the paperwork that you sent in. It's important to make any changes if there have been any," Sally said.

"Knock, knock," Alexa said as she and Tanya walked up.

"Hi, girls," I smiled at them. "These are my friends that brought me today."

"Come in and have a seat please. Kate, is it OK that I discuss your surgery in front of them?"

"Yes, of course," I nodded. Alexa sat on the edge of the bed and Tanya sat in the chair to my left.

As Sally was going over information, nurses came in to do a complete blood panel on me. The doctors needed to make sure that I was healthy for surgery with no infections. She had me sign the forms and then closed the packet.

"Next, I'm going to go through what you can expect the morning of surgery."

I nodded and tried to prepare myself.

"You need to check in at 8:30 a.m. and come to the same desk that you did today. You'll be taken to a room similar to this one and put on a gown. You may have guests with you but no more than about three to four at a time. There will be other people preparing for their surgeries and we don't like to have a huge crowd in the room in case they are loud and bother the other patients," Sally explained.

I looked over at Alexa who was frantically scribbling down what Sally was saying. She mouthed to me, *I'm taking notes.* I smirked and looked back to Sally.

She continued, "The anesthesiologist will come in and speak to you first and then they'll take you back. They will take some time to get you set up with the MRI machine, which will be live during the operation. You'll have a catheter put in and won't be awake during this. You don't want to see the operating room."

"I don't? Why not?" I asked hesitantly.

"It's a large room with many machines. It causes some people to panic just a little," she half smiled. "After they get you set up, they'll shave your hair where they need to first."

She plopped two bottles on the small table in front of me. "Wash your hair as you normally would and then wash your body with these. Don't use any lotions or deodorant after you shower. Also, no makeup."

I took the small bottles and set them by my purse. "Got it. What happens next?"

"They'll make an incision and peel your scalp down over your face," she spoke in a very matter of fact tone. Tanya quivered slightly and wrinkled up her forehead.

"A window-shape hole will be cut in your skull. The tumor will be dissected out. Your skull will be reattached with titanium strips and your scalp with be closed with stitches and staples."

I blew out a breath. "How much pain will I be in after all that?"

"Very little."

"Really?" I asked doubtfully.

"Yes, we take a lot of pride in keeping our patients comfortable."

"How long will the surgery take?"

"Each case is different. Probably somewhere between four to 12 hours. Please let your family know this so they aren't worried if and when the surgery goes long. Your designated person will have a pager that will keep them updated on your surgery. I see you have Josh listed?"

"Yes, that's my husband," I replied.

"Have him check in with the woman at the front desk as soon as he arrives in the waiting room. He'll need to keep her informed if he leaves so the doctor knows how to get ahold of him."

"Alexa, can you please tell Josh that in case I forget when you get here that morning?" I asked her.

"I've gotten it all written down," she smiled.

"Thank you. What else?" I questioned Sally.

"After surgery, you'll be immediately taken to the ICU. You may be there only 24 hours. It really just depends on how you're doing. Then you'll be transferred to another regular room."

Another nurse walked in and laid a stack of papers down next to Sally.

She flipped through the pages. "It looks like you're cleared for surgery," she smiled at me.

"I don't know if I should feel happy about that or not," I shrugged my shoulders.

"You're in the best possible place to have this done. The surgeons will get your tumor out and you'll be back on the way to being healthy again."

"Very true," I grinned at her. "OK, now what do I need to do?"

"Benjamin will take you down to do your MRI. They need to map it for surgery. Then I see you're scheduled later for a speech assessment."

"Yes. Do you think we'll have time to eat in between then?"

"Sure, it's a long test. I think you'll need to eat," Sally responded.

"Thank you for all of your help, Sally."

"My pleasure. Best wishes to you, Kate," she patted my hand and stood up. "Benjamin will take you down now."

THE MRI WAS very routine and what I was used to after having so many over the last year and a half. They scanned my brain for two hours and told me that those would be used in the operating room to act as a guide.

We had lunch across the street and I drank two sodas trying to get my headache to subside slightly. With all of the knocking and pounding that the machine had done and not being able to take medicine for pain, I was hurting. Next up was my scan to see where my speech was located.

Dr. T would be running my speech test. She had taken me to a small room first to explain about the procedure.

"So will I be talking during this test?" I asked.

"No, actually not at all. The test is run by showing you pictures of items and having you think what their names are in your head.

Different types of tests will be run and I'll watch for areas in your brain to light up while you're taking it." She flipped her computer around for me to see. "This is an example. You'll read in your head the instructions and then answer the questions in your head as well."

She pushed a key and words lit up the screen. "Name items that begin with the letter R. Begin in 3- 2 - 1. Go!" I read the screen and started running through R words in my mind.

"This next part is important. When it says to not self-talk, you'll need to quiet your thoughts. This will be like a reset for your brain in between the tests. Try and think of nothing during this time."

"OK. This should be interesting. I don't know if my mind is ever quiet!" I chuckled.

Dr. T grinned, "Just do the best you can. Should we get started?"

I followed her to another room with the functional MRI machine in it. She worked at positioning me just right so the goggles were directly over my eyes as I lie on my back.

"You'll be able to hear me giving instructions just like in a normal MRI machine," she spoke over the speaker. "Remember to answer all of the questions using only your mind. Let's begin."

I took a deep breath and blew it out. A black screen came up with words written in white.

"A series of images will appear. Think of the answers for each of these items," it read.

"Here we go," I thought. *"Sailboat, barn, dog, ocean, swing set... this is the easiest test I've ever taken."*

Next the screen lit up and stated, "No self-talk. Quiet your mind."

"OK, don't talk to myself. Dammit! I just did. And I did it again... be quiet. Ugggh." My mind was so loud I was worried that

Dr. P could somehow hear it and I was going to fail the test.

"For this next series, think of words that start with the letter O. Begin now."

"*O—alright. How about orgasm? Oh, shit! She's going to think I'm a pervert! Hurry, think of something else. OCTOPUSSY! Really? What is wrong with me?*" Worried that she somehow can hear these thoughts I laughed to myself. "*Change the letter please! Change it!*" I silently willed in my mind.

"Next letter will be a P. Think of items that begin with the letter P."

"*Oh, dear God!*"

AFTER ABOUT AN hour of doing exercises like that I was finally finished. Dr. T pulled me out of the machine.

"All done. That wasn't too bad, was it?" she asked.

I smiled, "Not too bad. When will you have my results?"

"Your surgery is Monday so definitely before then," she grinned. "There is a lot of data that was collected, so as soon as I make it through, I'll let you know."

"What happens if my speech is located on the right-hand side of my brain? Will they still do the surgery?" I asked.

"Yes, it'll just have to be done a little differently. Are you right or left handed?"

"I'm right handed."

"Most people have their speech on the opposite side of their dominant hand. We just want to be sure. I'm hoping that's the same for you and it's located on your left-hand side," she explained.

"Thank you for your help."

"You're welcome. I'll be in touch," she led me down a hallway and I walked out to where Tanya and Alexa were sitting.

I was so tired. My head hurt from looking at the screen for that long.

"Hey, how'd it go?" Alexa got up and walked over to me.

"Good, I think. She'll let me know when she has the results. I'm so tired and my head is killing me," I sighed.

"Let's get you home," Alexa put her hand on my back.

"I'm so glad it's over for you, girl. I have to head to Brae's basketball game. I'll text you later, k?" Tanya said.

I glanced down at my watch. It was already 4:35 p.m.

"I didn't realize it was so late! Thank you so much for coming and being here to support me today."

"Absolutely. I love you, sis." Tanya squeezed me and headed out the door.

Alexa and I got in her car and I laid the seat back to rest on the drive home. I closed my eyes, wishing that my head would stop pounding.

THE NEXT DAY was Saturday and my sister-in-law was flying in for the surgery. My brother, sister, and dad would come in tomorrow. Mom and I were sitting in a parking lot waiting for Shannon's plane to land and both of us were checking Facebook.

"No way! I didn't think she was real!" I gushed excitedly.

Mom looked over at me, "Who was real?"

"Amy. You know Target Amy? She just friend requested me. How did she find me when the name on my credit card is Catherine and my Facebook is Kate? Hmm."

I quickly accepted her and typed her a message about what our encounter had meant to me.

"I just got a text that Shannon is at door six," Mom said.

"I'll pull around." I put the car in drive and headed for terminal four when my phone rang.

"Hello?"

"Hi, Catherine it's Dr. T. I have the results from your test and your speech is located on the left-hand side. This is great news!"

"Oh, wonderful! Thanks so much!" I exclaimed.

"I'll send these reports up and they'll have them for surgery. Have a good weekend!"

"Thank you. You, too," I pushed the button to disconnect the phone. "My speech is on the other side. I'm so relieved!"

"Whew, honey. That's great news!" Mom said happily. "Oh, there she is!"

I pulled my car over to the curb and jumped out to hug my sister-in-law. Having her here for my surgery meant so much to me. She had pulled it off in only a few days and had found someone to watch her kids. My heart felt full being near her. We stayed up until 2 a.m. talking. My mom scolded me the next day for staying up so late.

"Who knows how long I have, Mom? I can sleep during surgery!" I smiled at her playfully.

IT WAS SUNDAY night and my entire family had made it to my house. My mom had planned an early birthday celebration for me. She made lasagna and as much as I loved that particular dish, I was having a hard time swallowing my food.

I kept looking around the table at Josh, my kids, and my family. I dropped my fork absently and it clattered to the floor. I had been dropping things a lot lately.

Each of my family members gave me a gift and a card. And with each card I read, I cried. I couldn't hold back the tears as I read what I meant to my family.

Would this be our last meal together?

My sister tried to lighten the mood by giving me an adult coloring book and a bell.

"I could've used this coloring book when I was doing the speech test and thinking of words that started with an O." We all shared a laugh but it was short lived.

I stayed up that night until two-thirty in the morning writing cards to my family. Usually, I'm on top of things but had been preoccupied the last few days with doing last-minute things for the kids to prepare them for when I wouldn't be home.

As I sat at my makeup table in my bathroom writing, I couldn't stop the fat tears that plopped down onto the counter. I listened to Josh snoring a few feet away from me. Normally, I was annoyed when he snored, but tonight I was cherishing his sound and synced my breathing to it. Slow and steady.

I crawled into bed and I prayed. I prayed for God to save me, for my surgeons to have careful hands, and for my kids to be all right—for me to be all right. I wanted to live. I wanted to be *this* same person when I woke up, and I begged God to not take my kids' mother from them.

When I finally drifted off to sleep, I was murmuring to God, hoping and praying that He heard me. That He would save me. Not only for the things I had left to do, but also more importantly for my children and what *they* had left to accomplish. My dreams couldn't end here... not tonight.

TWENTY-THREE

February 10, 2014

WHEN MY ALARM went off at seven that Monday morning, I was already awake just lying there. I slowly dropped my feet to the floor.

"What time is it?" Josh asked.

"It's seven. You're awake?"

"I didn't sleep much. How about you?"

"Nah. I didn't either. I'm going to get a quick shower and we need to leave at 7:45 a.m.," I explained.

"OK, babe. Do you need anything?"

"Yeah, more time."

Josh's lips curved slightly, "I know, bear. We'll get this surgery done and you're going to be so much better."

I nodded and slowly trudged to the bathroom. I washed with the special soap and took extra time to rinse out my hair wondering if this was the last time I would be able to run my fingers through it before it was shaved.

Feeling stupid for worrying about my hair, I tried to shake off that feeling. My hair would grow back, but at the same time, it was such an extension of me. It flowed down my back and clung to my wet shoulders feeling like a security blanket.

I dried off and pulled on my comfy pants and purple top. Drying and curling my hair was silly but I needed to be able to do it just one more time. I couldn't put any hairspray in it and so I just pulled it up into a ponytail.

Josh was watching me as I brushed my teeth. I smiled over at him with suds in my mouth and knew what he was thinking.

"Only positive thoughts, bear," he reminded me.

I nodded slowly and bent to tie my shoe.

"I'm ready. I'm going to say good-bye to the kids and then we need to go," I started to walk passed him. He grabbed my arm and pulled me to him.

"We're going to get through this together. I love you, Katers."

"I love you more," I pressed a kiss to his lips and went out into the family room where I could see my kids sitting at the kitchen counter eating their breakfasts.

"Kiddos. It's time. I need to go," I said, the words croaking out.

Tears filled my eyes quickly as I watched them slide off the bar stools and come over to me. I grabbed each one of them into a hug and kissed all over their faces.

"I love you so much. I'll be fine and home before you know it," I tried to reassure them but they all were crying and so was I.

"Kate, we need to go," Josh urged me.

"I know. Come here for one last hug," I knelt down so I was more at their level and held them all to me in one giant hug. Jillian was crying onto my shoulder and I could feel their warm bodies silently shaking against mine.

Taking my thumb, I wiped away a tear from Carter's cheek and tried to smile at him.

"I have to go. I love you so much, babies," painfully I pulled away from our hug and moved toward the garage door.

"We love you, Momma! We love you!" Chase yelled to me.

"Mommy, I love you!" Jillian's sweet voice was mixed with Chase's deep one.

"I love you, Momma! Two turtles!" Carter added in. That was always his ultimate amount of love was two of anything that he started saying when he was little.

"I love you more! I'll see you soon," I called and walked out the door into the garage.

Tears were streaming down my face and I took in a shaky breath.

My sister rubbed my back, "I know how hard that was. They're going to be fine. Do you want to sit in the front?"

"Nah. I'll climb in the back," I crawled into the bench seat in the back and looked around my car at my family. Josh and my dad were in the front, Bill and Liz were in the middle seats, and my mom was in the back with me. Shannon was going to get the kids to school and then head straight to the hospital.

My heart hurt. It was so full of love for my kids and the people that filled my car. I took a deep breath and breathed in their scents.

My phone started dinging with Facebook notifications and texts from just about everyone that wasn't with me. I didn't really talk on the long drive and let myself be distracted by answering all of the messages people had written on my wall.

"I got a text from Shannon. She sent me a pic of Jillian's hair all braided. Said the kids quieted down a few minutes after we left. She played 'Heads Up' with them and said they were laughing," I spoke aloud to the car.

"I'm glad. Shannon's so good with them," Mom responded.

The car was plunged into darkness as we moved through the tunnel signaling that we would soon be arriving at Barrow. My stomach started to churn, half from being hungry since I couldn't eat and half from nerves.

Josh pulled the car around the circle drive and let us out. My dad stayed with him.

"I'll be right up, babe," Josh told me.

I nodded my head and led my small group up to the fourth floor where I was to check in. It helped that I knew what to expect since I had just been here on Friday. The nurse took me immediately back and told me I could have three people in the room with me at a time.

"Go ahead and take off everything and put on these gowns. Put the first one on like a coat and then put your arms in first on the second one," she instructed. "I'll be back to start your IV line in a few minutes."

She pulled the curtain closed behind her. I quickly took off my clothes and put them in the bag labeled 'personal belongings' and set it next to the chair.

I grabbed the curtain and yanked it back and saw Josh standing there.

"Oh, hi. You were fast. Hey, can you go get my brother and dad please? I want them back here to listen to the surgeons to make sure I'm understanding everything," I asked Josh.

"Sure. No problem. I'll be right back," Josh turned and walked down the short hallway.

I climbed into the bed and covered myself with the beige blanket. I adjusted the socks that had little grippers on the bottom to help me from falling.

The curtain slid back farther and two nurses walked in.

"Hi, Kate. We're going to go ahead and get some lines going."

I nodded. Seeing my brother and dad walk into the room, I smiled at them. "You can sit down right there," I pointed to the two chairs. "Babe, can you grab another chair please?"

The nurses were tapping my veins in my hands and arms.

"We're going to start your IV in your left hand," she swabbed some alcohol to clean the area.

I looked over to where Josh had just taken a seat. "Hey, hon. You may not want to look," I teased him and winked.

"Oh, I'm not," he held his hand up to shield his eyes and looked sideways.

"How does that feel?" the nurse with the sandy blonde hair asked me about the IV in my hand.

"Actually it really hurts. I don't think I can stand to have it in for the rest of the week. Can you try somewhere else?" I asked.

Pulling out the IV, the nurse looked to the dark haired woman standing on my right-hand side, "Can you please check her right arm and see what we have to work with?"

I held out my arm for her to inspect the prominent vein that is always used when I have to give blood.

"This one will work," she tapped it and ran her finger down it. She pulled the tourniquet on it and then steadied the needle above my vein.

I turned my head to the left so I didn't have to watch.

"Uh-oh. We have a gusher," the nurse exclaimed and quickly was trying to get the blood stopped. It puddled on the floor and got all over my gowns and ran down my arm ruining my ID bracelets.

"Babe?" I called out to Josh noticing that he was suddenly gone.

"I'm right here!" he called from behind the curtain. "You're doing great!"

I laughed. "Good call. I don't want to have to move over in this bed for you when you pass out. It's a mess in here. Clean up on aisle four! Just stay where you are for a bit."

"Don't worry. I'm not moving," Josh replied.

I was given a new set of clean gowns, new ID bracelets, and they cleaned the small bed. After two more tries they were able to get the IV positioned and started saline.

"Your meds will be administered through your IV as well, as you will have another line placed on your chest as soon as you're asleep. You'll be hooked up to a lot of monitors that will keep a close eye on all of your systems during the surgery," the nurse explained.

"Can more of my family come back now?" I asked.

"Sure, that's fine as long as you don't get too loud," she replied.

"I'll go get them," Josh told me and headed back to the waiting room.

I glanced up at the clock on the wall and it was 9:30 a.m.

"Only one more hour," I said aloud, half to myself and half to my dad and brother.

"Look who I found," Josh said smiling.

"Oh, hey! I didn't know you were coming down!" I grinned at Reid, my neighbor and friend from when we were growing up.

"Hey, Kate. I thought I'd stop down on my way to work and see how you were doing," Reid explained.

"That's so sweet of you," Mom said to him. They started talking.

Shayla, Tanya, and Alexa were standing by my sister now, too.

I pulled the covers back and dropped my feet to the floor. Grabbing ahold of my pole with the IV, I stood and went over to give the girls a hug.

"Thank you all for coming," I smiled at each of my supporters.

"I can't stay long but wanted to come down and give you a hug," Shayla said.

"I'm so glad you did. I'll have Josh keep you posted."

"That'd be great! I hope it all goes well. I'll be anxious to hear."

"I hope to see you soon, girl. I love you," I hugged her again.

Shayla smiled and said, "I love you."

I watched her walk down the hallway and turned to my other girls.

"Hi."

"Hi, yourself. How are you holding up?" Tanya asked.

"Aside from this gorgeous gown and getting blood everywhere, I'm surprisingly

OK. Calm almost. I feel like God is with me."

"He is and will continue to be in the surgery," Alexa stated.

"I have to go to the bathroom again. Nerves," I wrinkled my nose and gritted my teeth. "Be right back."

I WAS BACK in bed again when the resident came in. His name was Dr. A and he said he needed to mark the side where my tumor was for surgery.

He walked over to my right side and marked with a blue sharpie a circle the size of a dime on my right temple.

"That's it?" I asked. "I don't know why but I was expecting something more technical."

Dr. A smiled. "The machines in the OR will be helping us out but we just want to make sure that we have the correct side."

"Makes sense. What now?" I asked.

"The anesthesiologist will be in shortly to give you some sedation or 'happy juice'. And Dr. S, Dr. Z, and I will be waiting for you in the OR," he glanced up at the clock. "I would expect them to come and get you in the next 10 minutes. See you soon," He patted my leg and left our small room.

I powered down my phone and handed it to Josh. "I can't believe the time is here."

"Good morning! I'm Dr. N, the anesthesiologist. I'll be taking you back and will be taking very good care of you during the surgery." He checked the computer and typed a few words then came over to my bed.

"Once I give you this happy juice you'll not remember the trip down to the OR. It works fast," he explained as he inserted the medicine into my IV.

I felt everyone's eyes on me and just like that it was done. He unlocked my wheels and started to push me out of the room. Everyone took turns hugging me and telling me they loved me.

I reached out my hand for Josh. He clasped it tightly and then we all stilled when a loud beep came over the sound system.

"Let's all pause for a prayer this morning..." a calm voice came on the speaker.

Perfect timing.

I prayed along with the voice and asked God one more time to be with me—to save me. When the prayer was done, Dr. N cleared his throat and I knew he wanted to take me down to the operating room.

Josh bent down to kiss me and I held him tightly in a hug.

"I love you so much. Tell the kids that for me. I love you," I whispered to him.

"I love you. It'll all be over soon. You're going to do great. I'll see you soon," he quickly pecked me on the lips one last time and our hold was broken as the bed started moving down the hallway.

The image of my family huddled in the hallway quickly became blurry as I didn't have my glasses on and the medicine was starting to take effect. Dr. N turned me and pushed me the opposite way from my family.

I talked nervously and watching as the bright lights overheard zipped by.

Why am I still awake? Was I going to be awake during surgery?

We came to the double doors leading into the operating room.

"Hey, Dr. N. I'm still awake. Just making sure you knew that," I said.

He chuckled. "I know you are. You've been talking the entire ride. Don't worry about it. You'll be asleep during surgery and won't remember this conversation either. Just relax."

The doors opened and it was very cool in the OR. There were so many machines and bright lights. I remembered the nurse saying that I wouldn't want to see the operating room. I didn't want to see this.

I silently prayed that I would fall asleep soon.

Please don't let me be awake for this.

"We're going to move you onto the table now, Kate. Can you lift your bottom up and move to the right?" someone instructed.

I just nodded and lifted my now heavy body. I felt dizzy and relaxed.

Inhaling a deep breath, I sighed and fell asleep.

I WAS IN surgery from 10:30 a.m. to about 6 p.m. Josh told me about those hours that I was asleep. After they took me back at 10:30 a.m., I was asleep while they were prepping me for an hour and a half. They positioned me and restrained my body and secured my head to keep me stabilized for surgery. The doctors removed the tumor from around noon to four o'clock. From four until about six o'clock, they would be closing me up by reattaching my skull with titanium strips, stretching my facial skin back over my skull, and sewing up my incision with interior stitches and 25 staples on the exterior.

My entire family, Tanya, and Alexa had stayed in the waiting room. Josh never left that room, not even to use the restroom, until he got the news from the doctor about how surgery went.

He held tightly to the pager that read 'Surgery in progress.' Around 4:15 p.m. he got a call from the surgeon saying that the surgery was over and they had removed a good amount of the tumor.

"Yes, but did you get it all?" Josh asked Dr. S.

"We feel comfortable with the amount we removed. We've sent the biopsy to the lab and will have the permanent findings in 72 hours. Right now, the frozen specimen says that the tumor is a most likely a Dysembryoplastic Neuroepithelial Tumor or a DNET. Only in 2 percent of people do these occur. If I were going to have a brain tumor, this is the type that I would want to have. We're going to close her now and once she's in recovery you can come see her."

"OK. Thank you, Doctor," Josh hung up the phone and quickly relayed the news to my family.

After an hour to an hour and a half passed, Josh glanced down at the pager that read 'Surgery in progress.' He was getting anxious and my dad and brother wanted to speak with the doctor to have some of their specific questions answered.

Alexa went up to the nurse at the waiting room desk and spoke with her.

"The family would like to speak to Kate's surgeon. They have some questions for him," Alexa stated.

The resident came out later and sat down with my family. They were able to ask questions about the surgery, my tumor, and my prognosis.

"We've just finished closing up Kate. She'll be in recovery in a few minutes and one of you will be able to go back to see her shortly," Dr. A told my family.

I SLOWLY OPENED my eyes and blinked a few times trying to get used to the dim lighting in the recovery room. Thoughts rushed through my head.

I'm alive.

I'm alive and I'm normal. I'm still me.

I could faintly see people moving in front of the curtain. I still didn't have my glasses on, and so all I could make out was a blur of movement.

I raised my right arm up in the air. I was tilted onto my left side.

"Hello? Excuse me. I'm awake," I half hollered half spoke to the person in the hallway beyond my curtain.

My head hurt. My back hurt. I reached up to the right-hand side of my face. My face ached. All of a sudden I felt nauseous.

"Hello?" I called again.

A beep went over the loud system and the calm voice came on.

"Good evening. Please pause for a prayer..."

I closed my eyes and listened as the voice spoke and I immediately gave my thoughts up to God praising Him for keeping me alive, keeping me the same, keeping me normal.

A nurse walked in quickly just as I said, "Amen."

"You're awake," she said as she moved to my left-hand side.

"Hi, yes. I feel sick, like I may vomit. Can you get me a pan or something?"

She methodically was checking my monitors and wires and

started typing something into the computer.

The nurse didn't understand my urgency.

"I need to vomit. Please, can you get me something? I don't want to ruin all of these wires and cords hooked up to me."

"You've had nothing to eat or drink, dear. I don't think you have anything in your stomach. Here," she handed me a wand.

I turned it over in my hand, "What am I supposed to do with this?"

"Place it in your mouth and close your lips around it if you need to vomit," she said.

Honestly? Has this woman ever thrown up before?

"That's not going to work. Seriously. Please, I need a bucket. Now."

She handed me a small pan that looked like it was supposed to be used for washing. I immediately vomited a large amount into it.

Oh, Lord. That didn't feel good.

"Oh. I guess you did have something in your stomach," she said plainly and took the vomit pan from me.

"Can you please bring that back after you empty it, just in case?" I asked her.

She nodded and walked out of the room. I couldn't keep my eyes open and drifted off to sleep.

IT WAS 6:26 P.M. and I peeled one eye open when I felt like I was being watched. Josh was standing over me with a huge, cheesy grin on his face.

"Hi, babe. Why are you smiling like that?" I asked him, reaching for his hand.

"Hey, Bear. You're good. The surgery went well!" He said, the smile never leaving his face.

"Yeah? What's wrong with me?"

"You have a DNET tumor. The doctor said that if he had to have a tumor, it would be the one he would want to have. It's pretty rare and found a lot in children and young adults. You may have had it for years."

"So I'm OK?"

"Yes, you're fine," he smiled.

"J, I remember everything. I'm still me," I smiled at him lopsided. "Ow. My head and face hurt."

"It will, babe. You just had surgery. Do you want to see it?"

"See what?" I asked.

"Your incision," he pulled out his phone and brought up the picture he had taken of me when he had first gotten to recovery to see me.

I tried to look at the picture out of the corner of my eye.

"I still have most of my hair!" I couldn't believe it. I had about a half an inch by ten-inch incision shaved to the scalp starting at my forehead in my hairline extending down a little past my ear in a crescent shape.

"I know. I couldn't believe it either. Are you getting tired again?"

"Yes. I love you. Please tell my family that, too. I'm going to close my eyes for a minute."

Josh stayed with me for about 45 minutes and told me later that he would repeat to me what the doctor had said about my tumor every time I woke up. He went back to the waiting room and showed my picture to my family.

Once Alexa and Tanya saw the picture and knew that I was OK, they left to go get my kids who were staying with our friends' Sandy and Bill. Sandy had picked them up from school and kept them. It was getting late, nearing eight o'clock, and Alexa and Tanya would get the kids from Sandy's and put them to bed. Alexa would stay with the kids until my family came home.

Every few minutes, a few more people would come in. Josh brought back my brother and Dad, and then Shannon and my mom came back.

I was vomiting again and later realized it was from the morphine they were giving me for the pain. Every hour they gave me morphine and I would immediately throw up. No one thought to change my pain meds, but it was definitely uncomfortable to vomit after brain surgery.

"Hi, sis," Liz walked over to my right side and Josh followed her into the small recovery room.

"Hi. Hey can you rub my back please? It's killing me."

She started rubbing my back.

"Dude. You know that you're rubbing my butt right and I'm commando," I said.

Liz laughed. "You're so skinny I couldn't tell it was your butt. Glad to see that you're the same. Already cracking jokes." Her cell phone started to ring.

She glanced down at the screen. "It's Chase."

"Answer it," I told her. "I want to talk to him."

"Hey, Chaser. I'm with your mom right now. She wants to talk to you," she handed me the phone.

"Hi, baby," my voice was weak.

"Hi, Mom! You sound funny. Are you OK?" Chase asked.

"I'm great. My voice is groggy because I was asleep for surgery a long time. I love you."

"I love you. Carter and Jillian are here, too."

"We love you, Momma!"

"I love you babies. I'll see you soon. Here's Aunt Liz." I smiled and handed her back the phone.

"I can't believe you just talked to the kids the night of brain surgery," Josh exclaimed.

"I'm so glad I did. Chase sounded relieved."

Liz hung up the phone and continued to rub my back. "I think we're going to head home soon."

I nodded and smiled with no teeth. "Remember when I told you I was going to tell Josh when I saw him the first time that I didn't remember who he was?" I asked Liz.

"Are you serious? I would've shit my pants, Kate," Josh retorted.

I chuckled, "It would've been funny, though."

I think it was that moment we all knew. We knew that I had made it. I didn't know yet that the surgery would be the easy part. I had no idea what the next 18 months would bring. But for now, I was alive.

TWENTY-FOUR
The first few days after surgery

MY FAMILY ALL went home, but Josh stayed as he was spending the night with me in the hospital. I was kept in recovery until close to midnight because they didn't have any rooms available.

The waiting room was now closed and Josh couldn't stay in recovery with me. He held his pillow that he brought from home and leaned against the wall right outside the double doors leading to recovery. He bent up his knees and slid down the wall sitting on the hard tile. He plopped his pillow in his lap and started checking messages on his phone. Checking in on work e-mails kept him busy until an orderly came to get him around midnight.

"Are you Catherine's husband?" he asked.

Josh nodded.

"We have a room ready for her. Come with me please," he instructed.

I was awake and knew that I was being transferred up to the ICU. As soon as the bed started to move I instantly felt nauseous from the movement.

"Please go slow. The movement is making me sick," I quietly explained.

After what seemed like forever we made it up to the ICU and they hooked up my bed to the monitors. Josh told me that he had stayed awake for a while once we got up there but soon crashed on the nearby couch in the room. He was exhausted after the very emotional day.

Every five to 10 minutes the nurses would come in to do a neurological check.

"Do you know what day it is?" the nurse asked.

"Yes, the tenth of February," I responded.

"What is your name?"

"Kate Mathias."

"Who is the president of the United States?"

"Obama."

"Very good. You can rest now," the nurse said and typed away on her computer.

At the beginning, the questions she asked were easy. They got progressively harder as the night went on. I drifted in and out of sleep, being awakened every 10 minutes for a test.

"What's 10 plus 10?"

"Twenty. Where's my husband?"

"He's behind you on the couch asleep," the nurse explained.

"I thought I heard him snoring." I couldn't turn my head to look.

"Why are you in the hospital?"

"I just had brain surgery."

"What day of the week is it?" she asked.

"Um, I think it's now Tuesday. Hey, I'm starving. Do you think I could get breakfast please?"

"They'll be taking you down to get an MRI soon. I'll order

you breakfast after."

They came around 5 a.m. to take me to get a post-op MRI. Lying in the tube with all of the knocking and pounding didn't feel good on my head or my back. Luckily, I had asked for more pain meds right before we went down. I promptly vomited them up.

My back was aching because of the position I had been in for so many hours for the surgery. Some moments it felt worse than my head.

I had just arrived back in my room when Dr. A came to round on me. Holding a pan filled with vomit on my stomach, I smiled lopsided at him when he sat down next to me.

"Did you just throw up?" he asked, his eyes squinting a bit.

I nodded. "I did. I vomit every time they give me pain meds so every hour. I started throwing up in recovery."

"No. You can't be vomiting after brain surgery. This is no good," he pushed out of his chair and immediately went to talk to the nurses. He was gone for just a moment and then came back in and sat next to me.

"They should've changed your medicine right away. I've prescribed a new one for you along with some nausea medicine."

"Thank you."

"How's the pain level?"

"It's OK. My back and jaw hurt, too," I explained.

"We had to cut your jaw muscle. Otherwise, your scar would've been on your face. We accessed your tumor by going in at an angle."

"Thanks for doing that, then." My scar is 10 inches and even though I would've looked badass with a scar on my face, I preferred to look the same as I did before surgery.

"I've given you muscle relaxers to help with your jaw pain. It should be better in a few days."

"OK. How long will I be here?"

"We'll get back the permanent specimen tomorrow and possibly then you can go home. It's a good prognosis. You'll have to be scanned for the next 10-15 years to check for tumor regrowth. There's a 30 percent chance that your tumor will grow back. Any other questions for me?"

"No, I think I'm good right now. Thanks."

He slid his chair back and stood up. "Dr. S will be by tomorrow to check on you. Get some rest."

The rest of that day was filled with family members. Some of them were flying home and so people were in and out visiting. By the afternoon, the talking was over stimulating me. My family's voices filled my head and overwhelmed me.

My sister must've sensed this. "How are you feeling, Kater?"

"I feel like I have fifty-thousand hammers are hitting me in the head."

"I'm sure. Do you want us to leave so you can rest?"

"I think so. Do you mind?" I asked.

"Not at all. I'll come back down later and spend the night with you. I want to give Josh a break."

"Hey, can I have my cell phone before you leave please?" I asked her.

She shot a glance over to Josh.

"Bear, you're not supposed to have a lot of screen time as it won't give your brain a chance to recover," Josh explained.

"I won't be on it long. Promise."

He handed me the phone and I powered it on. Instantly, messages began pinging.

My family left to go home and get the kids from school. I was tired but felt like I wanted a little outside contact with the world. I had a couple of texts from my cousins and friends. There were a lot of Facebook notifications but I felt too weak to respond to those.

I quickly answered the texts, one of them being to Randy. I had told him before surgery if he got a text with just random letters not to worry—that meant that I probably had just lost my mind.

I smiled to myself and thumbed a response.

Me: *XHJKSUFHFUIDJKKHD*

Randy: *(The laughing emoji) You're back! How are you feeling?*

Me: *I'm alive which is a bonus.*

Randy: *I'm so glad. Please take care of yourself.*

Me: *I'll be back to have you help me before too long. C u soon!*

I put the phone down next to me and easily fell asleep.

MY SISTER HAD stayed on Tuesday night with me and helped shower me in the morning. We couldn't get my hair wet for four days but she helped me to wash. I was a fall risk so had to have someone go with me to the bathroom. I'm a modest person but that went away when my sister had to help me to shower and dress.

My oncologist came that afternoon and had a lovely Scottish accent. It lulled me to sleep four times when he was speaking. Josh told me that he talked to us for 45 minutes. With all of the medicine I was on, I had a hard time staying lucid.

The part of the conversation I do remember is something

I'll never forget.

"Since we aren't sure if the tumor had indeed grown, you probably had between two to three years before you just would've died," my oncologist said. "You would've either had a large seizure or just would've died."

Two to three years? I'm only thirty-six. I have three small kids.

It was in that moment that I had a realization. Life is short. I could've died and soon. Over the course of the next 18 months I would realize a lot about who I am and who I would become.

I WAS RELEASED that evening around 8:30 p.m. just slightly more than 48 hours after I had brain surgery. I was amazed. When Josh had broken his leg a few years earlier, he stayed in the hospital for three days.

I just had brain surgery two days ago and they were sending me home?

I wondered if Josh and my family were equipped with enough knowledge to care for me. Worry and stress about being home and not under the constant eye of doctors and nurses filled me with a sense of panic. Then those thoughts would pass as my medication glossed over any rational thinking that I had.

We were going home, ready or not.

Unfortunately, the nurse that discharged me forgot to give me my pain medicine prescription. When we pulled up to the pharmacy window, she informed us that we needed the paper copy since it was a narcotic and it couldn't be faxed.

Josh turned to me, "Are they kidding me? You need your meds in 15 minutes." His voice was escalated.

"I know, babe. I'm hurting. Can you please call down to Barrow's?"

He pulled over in the parking lot and looked at the number on the top of my stack of prescriptions.

"Hi, yes. I just left with my wife and they said I need the actual copy of the prescription. Yes. Catherine Mathias. OK. I'm turning back around and will be there in 45 minutes. Please have someone down there with it ready for me. She just had brain surgery and needs her pain medicine." Josh hung up the phone and looked at me out of the corner of his eye.

"I'm OK. Just get home," I quietly said, carefully leaning my head back against the seat.

We were only eight minutes from home and that time went by in a flash since I had my eyes closed. My phone started ringing as we were rounding the corner on our street.

"I'm not answering that. It's Chase. We'll be home in 30 seconds."

No sooner had I said that then I saw my car coming at us in the other lane. Its lights were flashing at us signaling us to stop. Josh pulled up next to my car and stopped. He rolled the window down.

"Hey, where are you guys going?" Josh asked my dad who was in the driver's seat.

"Chase had a little accident. Can we get your insurance card?" Dad asked.

"Seriously? What happened?" I asked leaning over Josh.

Chase rolled his window down, "I was riding my bike waiting for you to come home. I ramped up on the sidewalk and my tire slipped in the gravel. The handlebar cut into my leg. Kris had to cut off my pants. I'm OK, Mom!"

I took in a big sigh.

My sister was in the car, too. "We'll be right back," she said.

"We're going to run him up to get a few stitches."

I shook my head. "Great," I muttered.

Josh handed them our insurance card and said, "I need to get her home. See you in a bit."

We drove the remaining 200 feet down the street and pulled into our driveway. I opened my car door and slowly climbed out. Kris was still outside pulling in his garbage can.

"Hey, Kris! Thank you for helping Chase tonight. Geez," I said.

"You're home? How are you feeling?" he asked.

"I've been better. They didn't send home my paper prescription so Josh has to drive back down there."

"Hey, Kris. Thanks for helping Chase. I'll catch you more later. I need to get her inside," Josh explained and slipped his arm around my waist.

I smiled at Kris and gave a small wave.

"Hope you feel better!" he called out to me.

"At this moment... I feel like I'm gonna die. I need my pain meds," I said over my shoulder as I started to walk into the house. I got settled on the couch and Josh took off for Barrow's to get my prescription.

I was on anti-seizure meds and a muscle relaxer for my jaw. I was also taking 20 milligrams of oxycodone every four hours. The doctor had told Josh that he couldn't write that on the prescription because the pharmacist wouldn't fill it, but those were my dosing instructions. I was taking four times the amount that Josh did after his leg surgery and I'm half his weight. No wonder I was struggling with pain now that it was wearing off.

Carter and Jillian came and snuggled with me for a minute on the couch, and then my mom put them to bed. It seemed like hardly any time had passed because I drifted in and out of sleep before Chase came back from urgent care and started telling me his war story.

"We were all outside waiting for you to drive in so we had gotten our bikes out to ride," he said. "My tire slipped and the handle bar jabbed into my leg. I almost passed out but Kris caught me. He laid me down and cut my pajama bottoms so he could see the wound. You know I always go commando at night with my pjs," he paused and smiled. "Well, I didn't want the girls to see my—you know what—so Kris was really careful cutting off the pants."

I grinned through my pain. Same old Chase.

"Thank goodness for that," I teased.

"So then Aunt Liz and Gramp took me to the urgent care and I didn't even cry while they stitched me up. Nine stitches. It'll be a cool scar, I think. Chicks dig scars!"

"Yeah they do. OK, lovie, time for bed. I love you." I smiled at him.

"Good night, Momma. I'm glad you're home," he trudged off toward his bedroom.

Josh got the prescription but by the time he made it back to fill it, the pharmacy was closed. He had to go to a 24 hour store and get my medicine. They only had a partial fill but he told them he would get the rest the next day.

That night Josh set his alarm and woke up to give me my medicine throughout the night every four hours. I was like an infant again. The medicine upset my stomach so I needed to eat before I took it. Mom put a bowl of grapes next to my bed to eat.

I had to sleep on my left side because of my head. I'm a right-side sleeper so that took a bit to get used to. My pain was well controlled as long as the medicine was given on time.

Thursday was a blur to me. I remember sleeping through the kids getting ready for school. I laid on the couch icing my head and slept off and on. I would fall asleep during peoples' conversations.

The amount of fatigue I felt can't be explained. My doctor told me that every extra bit of energy I had was going toward healing my skull and brain. That's why I slept so much. Also, when I was sleeping my brain could rest. I couldn't talk on the phone as the conversation was too loud in my head and would give me a headache.

Friday was my 37th birthday. I got up in time to give my kids the small gifts of Valentines before they went to school. Something I hadn't known if I would be here to do. As they left that day for school, I was emotional thinking about how blessed I was to still be here.

"Dad, I feel disgusting. Could you help me wash my hair?" I asked my dad. Mom had gone on a walk after she dropped the kids off at school.

"Sure. Should we do it in the sink?" he asked.

"I guess so. Let me go get some shampoo and conditioner," I walked back through the family room to my bedroom and had to sit down on my stool. I had no stamina or energy. I rested for a few minutes and then grabbed my stuff and took it back out to the kitchen.

My dad hoisted me up on the counter and I laid my head back.

"Don't get my incision wet but can you get out some of this blood?"

"Don't worry. I got it," he very lovingly held my head and let the warm water run down through the dried blood and crust left over from the surgery.

I've always had a special bond with my dad. I'm just as stubborn as he is and always felt better when I was sick when my dad explained what was wrong and that I would be OK. Having him wash my hair so sweetly reminded me of when I was a little girl. I felt secure and safe as my dad worked quietly on getting the blood out of my hair.

He had gotten most of it out of my hair but I still wanted to shower.

"Thank you, Pops. I'm going to get a shower now," I explained.

A SHOWER HAD never felt as good as it did that day. As the warm water pelted my back, I hung my head down and let it massage my neck muscles. They had braided a small portion of my hair right next to my ear. I assumed it was to keep my hair out of the way during surgery.

I pulled my hair to the side being careful not to get my incision wet. I started to unbraid it and the entire piece of hair came off in my hand.

I gazed down at the 8-inch hunk of hair in my hand and started crying. They had braided it and had obviously cut the hair when they shaved the rest.

My hair would grow back and I was lucky it hadn't been shaved as much as I had originally thought. I held onto that piece of hair and stared down at it limply lying in my hand. Water stained red swirled around my feet as more blood rinsed out.

My tears fell silently and mixed with the water so I couldn't tell the difference between the two. I wasn't crying about my hair... I was crying as a release that I had made it and was *alive*.

That birthday was and probably would be the best birthday that I would ever have. People laugh when I say that. Yes, I was drugged heavily on pain meds and had just had brain surgery—but I survived. I didn't know four weeks ago if I would live to turn another year older. I didn't know if I would live to watch my kids grow up, be a wife and mother, be a friend.

When I went in for surgery I had *hoped* that I would survive, but now I could say I did. And in the coming months, I would learn more about myself and the "new" me, because even though I thought I was the same when I woke up—I wasn't.

I was only four days out from surgery but I knew my life and who I was and would become was different. Everything was different. My perspective on living was different.

Life doesn't send out invitations. Don't wait. Take risks. Be unforgettable. Be happy and *live.*

EPILOGUE
Eighteen months later

IT'S AUGUST 2015, and I'm at my year and a half mark after brain surgery. I wish that I could say that the recovery has been a breeze and I'm living life the way I used to.

In April, three months after surgery, I started having partial seizures. I would have an aura right before the seizure so I would know a few seconds before it was coming on. An aura is a perceptual disturbance experienced by some before a seizure begins. I would have a strange fuzzy sensation in my head, my vision would get blurry, and often times I would smell odd odors.

The first seizure happened when I was driving home from dropping off Chase at football practice. I felt strange so I pulled over. During the seizure I would stare for up to a minute and lose the ability to speak and my body would feel paralyzed. Somehow I managed to drive home after it was over and texted my friend, Kellie, to see if she would bring Chase home. Josh was out of town and I collapsed into bed for four hours. Carter watched Jillian, and once I slept, I could function again.

I was still on anti-seizure medicine but they didn't stop these. With the next seizure I lost consciousness. I woke up feeling nauseous in the morning and went to the toilet to vomit. Jillian had come in to ask me something. I remember her standing over me.

"Mommy? Mommy? Wake up!" Jillian pleaded.

I was lying on the tile floor in my bathroom. I couldn't remember for a minute where I was or what had happened once I regained consciousness. My head felt like it might split open. My speech came out slurred as I tried to reassure her.

"Baby, can you get me my phone please?" I asked her still lying down.

She handed it to me and I punched in Shayla's number. I told her what happened and asked if the kids and my dogs could come over. Josh was at a meeting in Scottsdale and couldn't come home.

That day was a Sunday and I sent the kids over in their pajamas to Shayla's. She kept them for four hours. After they came home at one o'clock, my friend Sandy took them until 5:00 p.m. for me. I slept the whole day.

When I fell after that seizure, I hit my head and had a goose egg knot on it. Randy questioned me about it in physical therapy that week. I hadn't let Dr. Yu know about it. Randy pushed me to call the doctor after I hadn't told him about it for a week.

I went in immediately after speaking with Dr. Yu for a CT scan and had a concussion. It would be my first concussion of three in the next four months. My balance and coordination had been affected and I started to fall regularly.

The pain in my head was getting better but the nerves in my scalp had been severed. It felt as though a thousand knives were stabbing me in the head multiple times a day. If it wasn't hurting, it was itching, as the nerves tried to regenerate.

Next I started having vertigo and would have two episodes of

BPPV, benign paroxysmal positional vertigo. Randy is very skilled at what he does and was able to reposition the crystals in my ear to make the spinning stop. We videoed my eyes as they hopped and jumped up and down when I was having a spinning episode.

I plunged into a deep depression. I had fought taking an anti-depression medicine because I had never struggled before with sadness that overwhelmed me. I had never understood when people would say they were depressed. I thought they should be able to snap out of it. That's the problem—you can't.

The chemicals in my brain were imbalanced due to the surgery and some of my medicine also caused depression. I pulled away from society, family, and friends. I couldn't look at Facebook because I couldn't stand to see what everyone else was doing.

I cried all the time. Physically, there was an ache in me that I couldn't get to go away. I wished that I would die. I prayed that God would end this for me. Horrible thoughts filled my head... horrible, dead thoughts.

The awful irony of it was that as hard as I had fought to survive this surgery, now I wanted to be dead. The rational part of me, however, wouldn't allow these thoughts to take over.

My doctor told me I suffered from Post Traumatic Stress Disorder. Feelings of anxiety would overwhelm me until I couldn't function. I had trouble sleeping and when I would have pain in my head, I would automatically think the tumor was back.

I prayed. I prayed for help.

God, Josh, and my kids brought me back to life.

"The light at the end of the tunnel isn't an illusion; the tunnel is." I saw this quote by an unknown author and it rang true to me. I had so many things to live for—four bright lights—and I needed to show them that I was a fighter. This brain tumor wasn't going to beat me. *I'm a survivor and I chose to fight.*

The seizures lasted for four months the first time. I had a period of five months when they went away. They came back again in January of 2015, and I'm still struggling today with a different type of seizure. They're called "absent seizures" or *petit mals*. I'm managing them as best I can. They make me extremely tired.

I was having up to 20 seizures a day in January and February of 2015 and wasn't allowed to drive. My mom came out for three weeks to help me. I also used Uber to take the kids and me to sports and doctor appointments. The seizures are resistant to drugs, but they have lessened to about six to eight a day.

Part of the struggle has been—let's face it—financial. Many people have wondered what a surgery of this magnitude costs and if I'm still having financial hardships. Having a world-renowned brain surgery team isn't cheap. The surgeons and the facility alone were over 250,000 dollars. I'm fortunate to be covered under my husband's health group insurance plan with his employer. We had a substantial out-of-pocket deductible that needed to be met first. Once that was paid, I was covered financially 100 percent of the time. I would no longer have any co-pays for the subsequent doctor visits—there were many—or surgeries (I had sinus surgery 10 months after my operation and it was covered completely).

My medical bills would continue to flow in for about six months after surgery. No matter how good our insurance coverage was, any major medical event is always a financial hardship. But without it, it would have been a disaster.

With my filter gone, I swore like a sailor, which has some pretty funny stories that go along with it. My lack of judgment would cause me to say or do questionable things. My family has no trouble reminding me of those incidents and laughing about them now.

There was a period that I couldn't remember how to spell my

name. I couldn't remember simple words which led to great frustration.

I've had to wake up every day wanting to fight, even on the days that I didn't have the energy, to get back to the person I once was. I'll never get there but am happy with the new and improved Kate 2.0 version.

This is just a short synopsis of where I am in my recovery now. The second part of my journey, which is entirely about my recovery, can be found in *The Road to Recovery*, which will be released in fall of 2016.

THROUGH ALL OF this I feel so blessed. I wouldn't change having the brain tumor, as it's improved my life. People are skeptical when I say that but it has... it's changed me and everything about me, how I view the world, friends, and circumstances.

I used to be so OCD that when my kids would ask me to come and play a game or sit with them I would always answer, "In just a minute. I just have one more thing to do."

Now *they* are my 'one more thing'.

My children, when they're all grown up, won't remember that the house was always spotless but they'll remember what we did together and the memories we made.

We say that we're creating a moment. Life is full of moments... if only our eyes are open to them.

I've learned that sometimes certain people come into your life for different seasons. And it's OK to let some of those people go if they aren't adding to your life. I've found that I'm living on bonus time and have a second chance at this life; it's too short to surround myself with people that are negative and drag me down.

My experience has also taught my children that everyone is struggling with something even if they appear "normal". I look normal on the outside and no one would know what I am going through unless they asked. That's why I teach my kids to treat everyone with kindness and show them a smile. I tell my kids their smile may be *the* one thing that helps people that are having their own struggles get through the day.

Mark Twain said, "The two most important days in your life are the day you were born and the day you find out why." I've found out why.

I needed to be awaken from just *existing* in this life. I need to be present. Be here. Not just moving from one day to the next.

That's why today is called the present. It's a gift.

Our tomorrows are never promised.

My other 'why' is so that I can continue to share my story about my experience. If just one person finds comfort, strength or hope from my story, my journey will have been worth it.

I'm donating a portion of the proceeds from this book to the National Brain Tumor Society to help with research to find a cure. A cure can't wait.

And life won't wait either. So today I choose to live.

Make moments, laugh, be present, and enjoy the "gift" that today brings.

My story will continue in
The Road to Recovery
Coming fall 2016

ACKNOWLEDGEMENTS

This book has been a true labor of love for me. It took me nearly a year and a half after surgery to get it completed. It wouldn't have been possible without the grace of God and the patience, love, and support of many people along the way.

From the bottom of my heart, I'm without enough words to thank my wonderful husband, Josh. Babe, this journey has not been easy. Thank you for carrying me when I couldn't walk physically or mentally. You're my rock... my everything. I can't wait to spend the rest of my years growing old with you. I'm so grateful that is even possible. Thank you for never giving up on me. I love you... more.

My next three loves who have been so affected by my illness—Chase, Carter, and Jillian. You three are what inspire me daily to get up and fight. Thank you for all of the laughs, memories, and love you give me each day. You are my heart on the outside of my body.

Carolyn Chase—Momma, you saved us those seven weeks you lived with us cooking, doing laundry, helping with the kids, and taking care of me so Josh could travel again for work. I honestly don't know how we would've made it without you. Thank you for loving me unconditionally and always doing what's best for me. I love you so much.

My dad, Bill Chase, thank you for always being the calm voice of reason and helping me to realize that things may not always be what they seem. You're one of my greatest supporters and I'm so thankful to have you always on my side. I love you.

A huge thanks to my brothers and sisters—Bill and Shannon Chase, and Liz and David Todd. I lucked out the day that I got you as my siblings. Bill, thank you for coming to my rescue every time a medical problem came up. You're not only skilled as a doctor but also knew just what I needed. Thank you. Shannon, your thoughtful texts and verses always seemed to come at the exact right time and lifted me up. Thank you for being you. Liz, you've been one of my best friends forever and I can't put into words what our relationship means to me. I'll always look up to you, little sister, for who you are and what you're constantly giving to me. David, you've always been 'real' with me and I instantly felt a bond with you when you joined our family. Thank you for all of the support and kind words you always have for me. I'm beyond grateful for you all.

The words 'thank you' are simply not enough to convey what Dr. Kan Yu of Western Neurology deserves. I'm forever grateful to you for saving me. You continue to soothe and make every step of my recovery bearable. Thank you for never giving up on me until you found the right answer. You were right all along. You're the best person and doctor and I'm so honored to be able to call you those titles, along with "my friend."

To Dr. Randy Brimhall—Thank you for putting up with my sheer ridiculousness. You gave me back my life when you got my neck and back moving again. For each time you make my headaches disappear with a physical therapy session, I'm so grateful. Thank you for not only being my doctor, but also my great friend. Our belly hurting laughs have been so good for my soul.

Thank you to my in-laws, Mike, Suzi, Justin, and Casey Mathias. I'm so thankful that you were there to support me and especially Josh when we needed it the most.

For all of my extended family of cousins, aunts and uncles, I can't thank you enough for coming out and taking care of me, sending me messages and love, and all of the calls of support and encouragement. They say you can't choose your relatives but I wouldn't trade any of you for the world.

To my cover designer and truly awesome friend, Shelly Pratt, I thank you from the bottom of my heart. I look forward to our daily pictures, videos, messages, and voice chats. I've always admired everything about you. The 'new' me hopes to become more like you. Thank you for your unconditional love and friendship. xxx

Thank you to my amazing friends—my recovery wouldn't have been the same without you. I can't tell you what your text messages, flowers, cookies, meals that you brought over, rides to doctor appointments and my kids' activities when I couldn't drive, and phone calls meant to me. Thank you to my bestie Tanya Hoffman, Shayla and Kris Venkatesh, Jody Zvada, Kelli Patterson, Amy Ryder, Andria and Ryan Yoes, Laurie and John Rainey, Lee Ann Bohn and Dave Sperling, Franco "Kenpo" Mendoza, Angie Clark, Brynn Chase, Alexa, Alissa Sheldon, Shatha Nabboud, Sandy and Bill Mulholland, Denise and Jovan Kangrga, Sommer and Jason Skrnich, Martha Copley, Kellie and Todd Ostransky, Jordan Arjunan, Laura Bannister, Liz Fogle, John Wilson Nguyen, Reid Scholes, Shanna Overholster, Abby Schreck, Danielle and Tom Stull, Nancy Wright, Mia and Micah Kroger, Karen Scheffe, and Ryan and Corrin Scott.

And lastly but certainly not least, I thank my readers for sharing my journey. You may have bought this book because you are a fan of my writing or your interest was piqued after finding out this was not fiction, but a journal describing my physical and mental pain. Some of my struggles may be similar to your own.

When you purchased this book, I donated a portion of the proceeds to National Brain Tumor Society. There are 120 different types of brain tumors. Nearly 70,000 new cases of primary brain tumors will be diagnosed this year making the total more than 700,000 people that will be living with a primary brain tumor in the United States. Approximately 14,000 people will lose their fight this year from a brain tumor. Every day, nine children are diagnosed and more than 4,600 children between the ages of 0-19 will be diagnosed by the end of the year. I'm hopeful that this donation can make those numbers come down by helping with research to find a cure—a cure that can't wait.

Also by Kate Mathias
Worlds Apart
Hiding in Plain Sight
Spitfire

Made in the USA
San Bernardino, CA
11 November 2015